DELEGATION
THE KEY TO LEADERSHIP

Clay M. Cooper, PharmD

Delegation is the Rx
for successful leadership

Clay M. Cooper Pharm D

Cover Design: maxphotomaster (www.fiverr.com)

Back Cover Photo: Julie Martin, Enchanting Memories Photography

This book is dedicated to a myriad of teachers, professors, mentors, family, friends, and colleagues who have shaped me into the man I have become. Most importantly, it is for my wife, Emily, and my daughters, Claire and Eleanor, who continue to shape me into the man I aspire to be.

AUTHOR'S NOTE:

In this book, several terms are used to describe a delegator; the most often being "manager." It is important to note that while words may be used interchangeably, we are talking solely about one person: you, the reader. Whatever your station in life, the principles found herein can apply to many different scenarios. Take the information, apply it, and make it your own.

TABLE OF CONTENTS

INTRODUCTION

The idea for this book started when I was in pharmacy school. A friend of mine, Brian Marlow, was a year ahead of me in the program, and we both were in different leadership roles on campus. Brian was the president of the Pharmacy Student Government Association (PSGA), and I was president-elect of the American Pharmacist Association-Association of Student Pharmacists (APhA-ASP). I don't recall the exact conversation or what we were meeting about, but somewhere along the way Brian turned to me and said, "Delegation is the key to leadership."

Throughout the rest of our studies, we often repeated that phrase to each other, often in jest when we were swamped with tests, clinicals, organizational responsibilities, and fraternity parties. (Yes, your friendly neighborhood pharmacist was probably in a fraternity and more than likely has stories he or she would rather take to the grave.) However, it is an anthem that I have carried with me since that day and have tried, albeit terribly at times, to practice in both my professional and private life. Recently, I have come to some conclusions about my life, which I will share with you at the end, which needed to happen or else be resigned to be miserable. While doing this whole system reboot, "delegation is the key to leadership" kept reverberating in my head. It was time to explore this idea more fully if for no other reason than to quiet the voices.

I, like many of you, have read countless pages on leadership. I have been gifted several books on various ways, means, and methods on how to be a leader. Most often, these chapters pay homage to delegation but few jump into the deep end while the majority regurgitate the same themes over and over again. I'm sure there are some great books out there on delegation; I just haven't read them yet. I am not claiming to be an expert; far from it. I'm not really sure anyone *can* claim to be an expert on delegation, as we must all continue to develop and hone our skills on a daily basis. This book will be an education for me to see if I can practice what I preach and craft myself into a true delegator and leader. I hope it does the same for you in whatever way you find to apply these principles.

CHARACTERISTICS OF DELEGATION

"I don't have a problem with delegation. I love to delegate. I am either lazy enough, or busy enough, or trusting enough, or congenial enough, that the notion of leaving tasks in someone else's lap doesn't just sound wise to me, it sounds attractive."

— John Ortberg

Delegation has a variety of definitions, depending on who you are talking to. Delegation can mean that you bit off more work than you can chew and now are very desirous to move some of that work off your shoulders. It can mean that if you are careful, somebody else will get the blame if something doesn't go well. (The downside of that is that if it does go well, you'll have to find a way to garner the glory.) Delegation can mean that your manager wants you to do something for which you have no clue. You, in turn, pass it on to someone else who likewise has no clue but is fearful to tell you that. You'll find out it didn't work when the deadline nears.

I could start off this book by reading you Webster's definition of "delegation" or "delegate" but I really hate when other books do that; and, besides, it still does not get us any closer to an accurate description. The truth of the matter is that delegation means that you may not personally do the work, but may observe that the work is completed,correctly or incorrectly, and will be responsible anyway.

It has been said that if you want something done, give it to a busy person. The appellation implies that this person can somehow handle an increased workload or somehow has some superb ability to schedule the work. On the one hand, it is perceived, and often presented, as a great opportunity for the individual. On the other, a product not delivered will be perceived as a failure of the individual who accepted the responsibility, often without full knowledge of the ramifications.

We have all been in a situation, job, or organization where our time, talents and abilities are overtaxed. However, we often feel we will be perceived as weak or inadequate if we admit that what someone wants just cannot be produced in a desired time or volume. Many a person has cracked under the pressure of an overload, often brought on by one's willingness to tell others what they wish to hear.

If you do need help, you will obtain it only by being brutally honest, first to yourself and then to those who are counting on you. If you fear being censured, fired, dismissed, or "reorganized," and have adopted a "grin and fake it" posture, your time in the position is limited either through burnout or a failure to produce the anticipated results. Eventually, whoever assigned the work to you is going to expect you to deliver.

This, then, implies that if the work is to be done under your auspices, it must, by definition, be performed and accomplished by somebody other than you. If your people do the work, you will get the accolades. If you get the accolades, you must make certain that the credit is assigned where it is due and if there are bonuses or other privileges available because of satisfactory accomplishment, it is incumbent upon you to ensure that they are distributed.

The fact is always true that when your people perform and make you look good, you build the team's performance in concord. There will be enough times where the team misses the mark, and while you may take it on the chin for the failure, the reality is that for your people it must be a learning exercise. Fire, after all, is what tempers steel.

Theoretically, delegation means that as a manager, I have invited someone else to invest time, skill, and other resources in some work activity for which I am ultimately responsible and for which my career will rise or fall based on its successful completion.

Whether we wish to admit it or not, the hierarchical construct of most organizations dictates a sequence of personnel assignments. One president oversees two vice presidents, who oversee one or more division managers, who oversee several middle managers, who oversee floor-level supervisors, who, in turn, oversee the workers actually performing the work. Granted, efforts to flatten the organizational chart will continue where there is downward pressure on profits, but the fact is that in any organization—structured or voluntary—there is a downward movement of task assignment. There may be minor adjustments for organizations that are structured as networks.

There must be some characteristics of delegation that can be applied to obtain the best results. Consider these:

- A manager is placed in a position of responsibility for one or more tasks or responsibilities.

- The manager is, by definition, responsible for more work that he or she is individually capable to perform.

- For the task or process to be suitably handled, the manager must have the authority to commensurate with the responsibility that has been assigned.

- The assignment of responsibility without the commensurate assignment of authority to affect the outcome implies a weakness in level-to-level management communication.

- Delegation may imply either total or partial assignment of either responsibility or authority. That may apply to either a complete process or task or to a very specific single task.

- Delegation may be a form of representation on behalf of a manager or an organization, but carries with it the encouragement and authority of the delegate to act on behalf of his or her sponsor.

- Delegation implies a leader and a follower, where the leader may *have* the ultimate responsibility for the completion of the task and the follower the responsibility to select *how* the task is completed. Deadlines may be imposed or negotiated.

- Delegation is a shift in decision-making, moving action authority lower into the hierarchy and/or network form of organization. Thus if a manager perceives that his position and recompense is tied to having his or her finger on the pulse of every action and every decision, there will be reluctance to delegate anything at any time.

If it is true that the one who delegates—the person who assigns work—is responsible for that work (and it is) it would behoove such a delegator to establish routines of trust, avenues of communication, and suitable recognition or award for the correct performance of the specific tasks.

Effective delegation implies "give and take." It is not an abdication of responsibility, for a higher level of management will hold the delegator ultimately responsible. It is not its antithesis, micromanagement, where the delegator "bird dogs" the entire process for lack of trust of a subordinate and a fear that there is just too much at risk to assign the work to somebody else.

A leader who micromanages, e.g., one who oversees every detail of a task he or she has assigned to another, fails to develop the team. Teamwork is inherent and necessary for the accomplishment of any delegated task.

Properly done, delegation gets the work done, builds skill in your team, builds cohesion of the organizational unit, and provides the training that will permit subordinates to advance, perhaps in another part of the organization. A manager who can do this well will motivate his or her subordinates to perform with excellence. Excellence, in turn, pushes an organization along in the successful accomplishment of the unit's goals.

Poorly done, the situation will lead to incomplete work, frustrated people, finger pointing, the ducking of responsibility, and jobholder turnover.

The implications of delegation carry some "must haves":

- The assigned task or process must have some very explicit goals and objectives. A goal (get it done) is different from an objective (the result of successful accomplishment). The third element (when is it needed) somehow becomes the motivating force. There is a very fine line between "get it done" and "get *something* done." There is an equally fine line between "on time" and "as soon as possible."

- The person or team to whom the work is delegated must have the skills necessary to perform the work. If the skills are not present, then training must be accomplished, and it must be accomplished apart from the time allocated for performing the work itself.

- The plan for delegation must be executed. Task lists must be prepared. Skills must be trained, obtained, or shifted to accomplish the delegation. In some cases, a specific person must be trained to a specific task, plus some effort must be given to train a second individual to assist in the primary assignee's absence. Inherent in such a plan will be the need for realistic staffing. It seems logical that if a work group is already tasked to an acceptable percentage of available time or duty that the imposition of more work without the availability of more resource would seem counterproductive. In short, for a significant delegation there must be a significant amount of preparation for all parties involved.

- The person doing the delegation must be willing to be held responsible for something over which he or she may not have absolute control. It is reasonable to assume that the delegator will put in place those reports, performances, and verifications necessary to ensure that the delegated duties or tasks are indeed performed as planned.

- The person doing the delegation must be willing to divorce himself or herself from the "nitty gritty" of the task, even though that task may be more interesting than other tasks for which the manager is responsible. Sometimes it's more interesting and fun to "work on the new project" than it is to assign it and merely monitor its progress.

- The person doing the delegation must be so familiar with the generalities of the task or process as to be able to detect, hopefully in advance, when it is about to run off the rails.

- Delegation requires regular and frequent progress measurement. That measurement must be done in a manner that allows the person doing the work to take corrective action in time to prevent any negative results or incorrect decisions. That implies a plan, a structure, and adherence to them both. Harvey Gollub, who once led American Express, made this observation: "If a project is allowed to change freely, the rate of change will exceed the rate of progress."

• The manager and his hierarchy must accept the fact that a change in project specification will involve an extension in time and perhaps even a change in resource, particularly where the deadline may have been accelerated, hopefully for some valid reason.

• The manager (delegator) and the employee (delegate) must understand that the plan must be met, and if that is not possible for a valid reason it is the *plan* that must be changed. Reclassification of priority may be a perquisite of higher management, but somehow the expectation of performance on other displaced or delayed tasks often never is changed.

• The manager who wishes to delegate must recognize that time itself is a finite resource and his or her time in particular has a maximum "stretch." Realistically, any employee's value to an organization is measured in contribution to profit per unit of time or work expended. It therefore follows that the manager, whose per unit of time or work has a higher impact on profit, must in every case evaluate the productive and efficient use of time versus the time of a capable subordinate.

The economic concept is called "elasticity." In the simplest of terms, this is how much of one action must be set aside to permit the performance of another action. That must be evaluated in terms of productive output per unit of time, what the economist calls "the production possibilities curve." Therefore, the one who is to do the delegation must recognize the per unit exchange of outputs among the various people available to do the work.

• The manager who delegates must accept the fact that somebody else may be able to do the task or process as well. That is, however, a golden ideal, largely because we seldom stop to evaluate the scope of what we accept to do. That implies that not only should the work mix be evaluated when a new task is pondered, the work mix should not be accepted unless it can be proved possible with the available time or staff.

- It would be fair to say that to successfully delegate, the manager must set ego aside. He or she must accept that the work unit rises and falls on the efforts of everybody who is assigned. Further, the manager must function as the funnel—the place where the work is carried (and any—and all—communication relative to its performance). For a manager to delegate a task and then take himself or herself out of the loop begs for the project to expand without controls and perhaps even without limits.

  It is also fair to say that during the first ever delegation of a given type, the manager may well be sitting "on pins and needles." To begin with, he or she may literally not know how to do the task. If the task isn't described fully or if the manager is simply willing to tell his superiors what they wish to hear, there is a large risk for the project to get away from the person to whom the task was delegated. It follows that if your boss gives you a task that you don't know how to do, you in turn give it to me, and I'm not sure how to do it, by virtue of the hierarchical structure, I may not tell you that. I may not even know that I don't know how to do it until I've dug into it. Until I am confident in the work—until you are confident in my work—I would highly recommend that you make no commitments that may be impossible to achieve.

As a manager, my delegation of a task to anyone is a recognition that in reality, my boss may not need me—at least as relates to this one task. Every manager who delegates work is training a replacement. The sooner you recognize and accept the fact, the better you and the organization will be. Your management isn't about to promote your replacement based on a single task, so get over it. In the same manner as you are responsible for more work you can physically perform yourself, you are responsible to be the focal point of many projects performed by many subordinates, drawn together under your aegis, and presented to your superior as the effort not of you, the manager, but of your team. You want success as a delegator—that's where it lies.

That's fine, but some will say it is shortsighted. To begin with, not everything can be delegated. You would not want to delegate to Employee A the performance decisions that must be made relative to Employee B, for example. Peers may judge performance among themselves, but should not maintain management functions between them.

There are other considerations, as well. Is there the possibility that the new task will become a recurring assignment? If this is true, assigning it to existing staff is prima facie evidence that people have been wasting time and that the new assignment will fill the wasted hours. That might be true for minor tasks, but major tasks imply the availability of major chunks (or slices, if you will) of available time. People may be willing to accept a work overload for a short period, but not necessarily over the long haul. Time-and-a-half wages are a suitable incentive, but nobody wants to do that forever, even if the time is paid time. More troubling is that many office people are not on the clock and are therefore subject to abuse, often enforced by guilt-trip suggestions of heightened positions.

How critical is the task? Is there a person on your staff who has relevant skill, current knowledge, or intense interest? If there is, could you clear the other work for this person while he or she takes it on? If so, how would you distribute the work that has been removed from that person?

Is there time to do the task? Are you interested in effective performance, efficient performance, or simply "quick and dirty" performance? If there is not time to train for the task, have you the authority to seek help outside the organization? Is there budget that will permit that? A similar situation exists with recruiting for the position. If you recruit for this task alone, will you be faced with having to recruit for other tasks, or is there some transference to be obtained?

An old maxim of project management goes this way: "if you don't have time to do the thing right, how will you find the time to do it over?" If you are to delegate work, you need to know that it can be done within the constructs of the project, what flexibility (or elasticity) is available, and what the consequences are for either an incomplete task or one not completed within the allowed timeframe. One thing you will notice is that every level downward a task is pushed, the amount of built-in "fudge factor" is decreased. Therefore it follows that the planning and plan revision is an ongoing process that must be followed religiously to avoid several tasks becoming equally critical. On projects of significant size, the one doing the delegation must establish, monitor, control, and adjust a critical path.

In the 14th Century, some wise man posited this little ditty:

For the want of a nail, the shoe was lost.

For the want of a shoe, the horse was lost.

For the want of a horse, the rider was lost.

For the want of a rider, the message was lost.

For the want of a message, the battle was lost.

For the want of a battle, the kingdom was lost.

All for the want of a nail.

On its surface, the message is that small actions can result in large consequences. That's a given. For the modern organization, however, it should convey the concept that from top to bottom, each level of organization management must depend on the one(s) beneath it. The message is simple: delegate down all you wish, but recognize that performance must be upwardly dependable.

Which bring us to the final characteristic of delegation. I can delegate until the cows come home but the person accepting the delegation must accept the obligation. Unless that individual is willing to accept and commit to the complete performance of the task—giving due consideration to each element herein presented—then nothing other than disappointment will result. That disappointment may well result in the loss of opportunity, competitive position, or the very important contribution of the delegated task or process to the overall mission of the organization itself.

This beginning chapter is a prelude for the rest of this book. Not only have we defined delegation and illustrated its characteristics, we have also introduced several key words, phrases and ideas that the rest of the book will now expound upon. We have outlined a process for becoming good delegators and ultimately good leaders.

WHAT IS APPROPRIATE TO DELEGATE

"Don't be a bottleneck. If a matter is not a decision for the President or you, delegate it. Force responsibility down and out. Find problem areas, add structure and delegate."

– Donald Rumsfeld

Delegation no longer simply means getting work done faster or shirking responsibility; delegation has evolved into what can be a symbiotic process whereby the person taking on a new responsibility or task is empowered in the process, while the delegator achieves more than he or she would without assistance. To delegate well, you must have the right task and the right person, which takes more than guesswork. It's equally important that you are able to explain the task and set concrete expectations. Even with the right person for the job, delegation does not equate to autopilot. Once you have delegated, creating checkpoints for extensive tasks ensures that you still evince leadership while confirming progress on the delegated task. Though there is an element of trial and error, there are simple guidelines that can create a successful partnership through delegation, which we will examine in detail.

When faced with not only the normal tasks associated with a job duty but additional projects, delegation needs to happen. The difficulty is first in determining what to delegate. The first step to successful delegation is to g*et organized*. This step will involve a time commitment, but once you set up your system, it is easily maintained. This text isn't a book on organization, but this step is a vital process in many ways. Getting organized applies to not only an individual project or task, but your overall workload and schedule. In addition, you have to consider the available workforce, accounting for vacation time, holidays, and the current workload of your team, all of which require organization. When you make an effort to account for all tasks and items that are required of you, naturally you can start to assess which need your personal attention and which can be redirected if time is not available. The best defense is a good offense, so be prepared for unexpected obligations, and you will avoid being surprised.

Once you understand the workload in front of you, examine the deadlines for each item and estimate the time commitment to complete each project, leaving spare time for any necessary revisions or changes. Prioritize your responsibilities based on the following questions:

- What needs to be completed the soonest?

- How long should the task take?

- Is this something that is absolutely in your job description, or is this an extra project?

- Is the information sensitive?

- Could you complete the task in five minutes or less?

- Could someone else complete this in a reasonable timeframe?

- Are you staffed to be able to have someone take on this task?

Based upon your role, the current work climate, and your team, some questions may be more important than others. Generally, tasks that are secretarial in nature and involve your employees' information should be completed by you, but can be done at various times of day. Choose a timeframe when you tend to have less demand on you, to quickly complete these tasks. For anything that is secretarial but doesn't involve security concerns, the thought process changes: if you can complete a task more quickly than your employees and it's a small time commitment, consider the deadline and other obligations you have. Chances are it will benefit you to train someone to take on the task, as it will save time in the long run. However, if your team is overwhelmed with work, complete the item yourself and set a short meeting to later show an employee how to perform that function. Generally, if your team is overextended, it saves time to complete these easy tasks yourself in the moment, rather than explain the process. That type of delegation should be left for times when you have more flexibility in your schedule to devote to developing your employees and increasing their repertoire or knowledge.

Besides essential managerial functions, one of the most important and often overlooked aspects of your workload may be employee feedback and coaching. Reviewing employee ratings and formal evaluations should always be a task that you handle personally. Coaching or performance improvement can be delegated. The difference is that you need to present the "what", as this relates to performance and salary. Other employees can provide the "how", which is technique and skill set. This is an instance of the symbiotic nature of delegation. In this case, three parties are benefiting from the dispersal of authority: the employee needing feedback gains coaching and support, the employee providing feedback gains confidence and experience in coaching, and as the manager you provide performance support and developmental opportunities, while effectively managing your time.

Deskwork and general management duties have been outlined, but there are also the extra projects and tasks that arise which may require delegation. Deadlines can be long or short, or often ongoing, in that the task involves consistent meetings or conference calls. Consider the timeline but also the time commitment, as well as the objective of the group. Also think about the microcosmic pieces that go into the project as a whole. Are there menial tasks that involve fact finding, creating a document or template, or gathering information? Those aspects of the project can be time consuming, but if the content is not classified from agents, can be appropriate for delegation. What is done with the content, or higher level analysis may need to be done at the leadership level, but delegating the menial tasks saves time that can be spent on extrapolating meaning from the data gathered.

Does this mean that we should only delegate menial tasks to subordinates and keep the "big important" job for ourselves? By all means, NO! This is just a stepping stone to get you thinking about the delegation process. One key aspect of delegation is growing the abilities of those around you. While the examples used in this book may seem trivial, knowing your team, which we will discuss later, allows you the opportunity to hand out more and more critical projects. Many menial assignments can be universal across organizations and allow for applicable examples, but they are not a stopping point for delegation but rather a starting point.

In other instances, there will be projects where you are on a team with your peers, and employees cannot be utilized. Consider the division of work amongst the group. If you are apt to volunteer for every task, you will find yourself overwhelmed. In groups where a peer has the same knowledge or skill set but no task, delegating horizontally may be a great option. It represents initiative on your part to manage your time, as well as teamwork but a sense of accountability to distribute responsibilities. When you become a resource for projects, it is easy to lose time managing your employees, which is a key aspect of your job description. Part of delegation is to understand your priorities and goals. If you want to advance in your career, the recognition of working on a project can be helpful, but a successful team is its own recommendation. Projects can often supply a much-needed change of pace, but once the project is done you need your team to be performing well, as you are accountable for those results. This creates the balancing act that necessitates delegation.

Whenever we delegate a task or even consider the possibility, there can be slight hesitation or fear of losing ground in the objective of career advancement. The misconception is that the more items you take on, the more invaluable or remarkable you become. In truth, managing your workload, using delegation with discretion, and knowing when to say "no" are hallmarks of great leaders. Not every opportunity is going to benefit your long term goals. There may be some that you accept because you believe in the objective, which is fine. However, the confidence to share responsibility highlights a strength and sense of self-worth that are more impressive than the juggling skills required to never disperse tasks or share projects. Delegation, when done thoughtfully, is not a weakness. Most managerial roles assume that some dissemination of tasks will take place; the actual principle being measured is how you best leverage your time and people, given the responsibilities at hand. It is essential, then, that we come to recognize delegation is not an admittance of failure—it is an opportunity to show management skills and incisive judgment to achieve more than one person would be capable of.

It can also help to know each of your employee's unique skills. This can be as simple as observing strengths in your team, or can delve deeper by asking agents to define in their own terms what they bring to the team. Cataloging the various assets will make delegation much simpler, and can more easily answer concerns about completing a task in reasonable timeframes. As a leader, delegation will not shift any of the accountability for a project's outcome. Therefore, you not only need to understand your workload to be successful, but you must also have a keen insight into each of your team member's strengths and opportunities. If the task fits and the skill set is evident in an employee, the risk of delegation is decreased. For example, your Microsoft Excel aficionado is a safe bet to complete data entry and develop formulas. For more ambiguous or creative assignments, successful completion is harder to achieve and will depend upon solid communication, as well as the ability of another person to interpret your vision. Crystal versus fluid knowledge will come into play, based upon the type of assignment needing delegation. An employee whose strength lies in words and interpersonal interaction, as opposed to numbers, is ideal for client-facing tasks, such as focus groups, live interviews, or other communication-based tasks. Within the same project, there may also be a need for entry and analysis of the data gathered, where more crystallized thought processes bring order and logic to the masses of information. Delegation will require the insight to appropriate not just a whole task, but even smaller portions to best leverage the skills of your team. Knowing where those skills lie engenders appreciation among your group for offering extra opportunities, bolsters confidence when tasks are appropriately doled out, and unveils your critical thinking and management skills.

One final point to consider is the morale on your team. Delegating all extra work to one person can create ill feelings and produce concerns about favoritism. This can be addressed in two parts. The first and perhaps most key piece in delegation is communication. Let your team know who was chosen for a task and why, especially for long projects where it's clear that the agent is not working on normal items.

Explain what criteria you used to make the decision and why the person fit those needs. Many managers feel that they don't need to justify themselves and distribute tasks on the fly, but the results speak for themselves. If you explain the skills you are looking for, employees will evaluate themselves against expectations and this can produce performance improvement. It also squashes rumblings of the age-old "teacher's pet" jealousy. Consider any role or task you applied for and were not awarded—would you rather know why it was awarded to someone else or conjure up those answers in your own mind? It's a pretty safe bet that transparency will be much more accurate than imagination in these cases. The other consideration is to *spread the wealth*. As a person who was on the receiving end of a large number of projects, it can isolate you from your peers. Everyone appreciates a break from monotony, and knowing your team or recognizing who may mentally or physically need a change of pace is also essential in successfully leading your team. There will be times when you delegate based on determining who can complete the job satisfactorily, although they may not be your first choice, because of extenuating circumstances. Managing not only the skill sets but the morale and mood of your group elevates a manager to a leader, but again it requires communication.

Overall, this is the ideal breakdown of how delegation should take place. There will be times when the ideal process is not possible. Attrition can decrease the number of workers and cause other tasks to be assigned without notice. Prior to an organizational structure, deadlines can creep up and the ideal candidate for delegation may be unavailable. In those instances, judgments have to be made. Again, evaluate the priority of the tasks at hand: which deadlines are soonest, what is the time commitment, and can someone else complete this successfully and in a reasonable timeframe? If the situation does not allow for a finished product that you are comfortable being responsible for, delegation to your team may not be an option. We will evaluate other avenues and options in later chapters. It is essential to understand that although a task may qualify for delegation, circumstances can often complicate achieving that objective satisfactorily.

In addition to extenuating circumstances, there may be one final aspect of an assignment that complicates whether to delegate: your feelings about the task. If you are on a committee and suggest a process improvement that is your brainchild and incites passion in you about your work—that's significant. Tasks that take a time commitment but pay dividends in job satisfaction are not to be undervalued. If you can own the project and gain enjoyment from the outcome of your labor, that's the ideal situation in any workplace. Let's examine that opposite situation—an assignment that you are ambivalent toward. It's important to understand why the task was given to you. Does it involve a specific skill set only you possess? Is it time sensitive and in need of your organizational skills, or does it seem like busy work—a task that needs to be completed but anyone could accomplish? This is where an open conversation about the scope and goal of the task will help you understand if this is something you can delegate to a subordinate, or holds more importance than you may realize and will benefit you to complete on your own. If your analysis of the task is that the job can be done without specialized skills, confirm that you are happy to help with the project and were thinking of including so-and-so; if your supervisor is in agreement, excellent. It's important to present the situation not as a conundrum needing outside help, but as an opportunity that you, as a leader, are sharing with your group.

There is one final scenario which may not immediately suggest a need for delegation, but instead creates an opportunity for testing your team's skills in a less deadline-driven way. Those are the tasks that have indefinite completion dates or that are recurring and don't require a manager to complete. This may be something as simple as accounting for all occupied space in your department or confirming software updates—the task is detailed enough to require some time commitment and will be a recurring assignment, but has some flexibility in the completion timeframe. Because of the flexible timeframe, some leaders may take this on as a duty to be fit in as scheduling allows, but the nature of the assignment is not specific enough to require a manager's attention. Don't fall into the trap of trying to maintain tasks simply because the deadline is fluid—consider the skill set involved and allocate to your team. It's a morale boost and change in the daily workflow that can offer a needed break to your direct report, and allows more time for duties that are specifically managerial in nature, as well as unexpected situations that demand your attention.

Implementing organization into your daily work life not only allows you to determine which tasks to complete when—it delineates your entire workload, and can provide a platform to contrast tasks that require your direct attention versus those that can be delegated. However, knowing your team is the only way to delegate successfully, as the right task with the wrong person will either hinder completion or degrade the final product. Clearly the process of delegation is more about smart choices and careful analysis than a black and white decision. Make sure to consider the following to maximize your work time and results.

When Assessing What to Delegate:

1. Organization is the best way to prioritize tasks and assess what can be delegated.

2. Evaluate not only the tasks that need to be completed, but the workforce availability and impact to other job duties for potential delegates.

3. Know your team (*including yourself!*)—assign tasks with a mindfulness for the skill sets each person possesses.

These three concepts serve as the backbone for the rest of our discussion on delegation. They may seem very simple and many may say "Oh, I've got that down; let's get to the important stuff." However, if these ideas are not at the forefront of any decision made regarding delegation, the entire project may crumble or, at the very least, limp along to a subpar "success." We will revisit them often and use them as cornerstones as we continue.

WHO TO DELEGATE TO

"The greatness of a leader is measured by the achievements of the led. This is the ultimate test of his effectiveness."

- Gen. Omar Bradley

With a basic foundation of what to delegate, we can now examine finding the appropriate party for delegation. This can include your employees, peers, and your boss, and often a mix of the group, depending upon the scope of a project. Most often delegation is thought of as transferring a task to a subordinate, but in the leadership world, assessing the most appropriate personnel for a task is equally as important as knowing what to delegate.

When delegating to employees, it is understood that a basic knowledge of strengths and unique skill sets will suggest the most appropriate person for the role. Technically savvy employees can be utilized to help others learn new software, to troubleshoot technical issues, and to coordinate system updates, ensuring all employee machines are operational. These employees likely have strong logical minds, meaning they are also ideal for tasks involving concrete steps or formulas, including data entry. That being said, you will have other employees who, although less technically savvy, are capable of data entry, as it is a repetitive task. It's important to evaluate not only the candidate who can most easily complete a task, but who else can accomplish the objective satisfactorily, as this allows for greater division of labor and provides opportunities for everyone. These types of assignments, though necessary, take up time that could better be used for other management duties and don't require managerial experience —meaning they should not be reassigned to a peer or senior management. In general, data entry not involving personal or sensitive information should be delegated to subordinates, as it is not a complicated task but can require a disproportionate time commitment —simply said, it's one of the tasks that have to get done but don't require a special skill set, other than typing.

Given the spread of skills in the current work environment, it's worthwhile to evaluate typing as a skill. Millennials can scarcely conceive of a person unable to type; however, for many workers with seniority, computers have not always been a given in the workplace. Work that previously may have been done in hard copy is likely now completed electronically, and this transition has left a divide in computer skills. It's important to be aware of this divide, should it exist amongst your employees. Assigning data entry to an employee who relies more on "hunt and peck" than the "home row" will likely result in a noticeably slower finished product. Ask yourself—is it worth the time commitment to use this task as a typing exercise, or does the current workload require faster results? Consider the other tasks you need to delegate. Someone with exceptional communication skills but less than stellar computer skills may be an ideal coach. Consider, too, the temperament of your employees. Managers often avoid utilizing jaded employees, but it's important to address and then motivate, which can be done through delegation. Be sure to offer concrete expectations for the tone of coaching; it can be leveraged as an opportunity but emphasize that the outcome will be assessed, creating accountability for the coach to perform as expected. This also relates back to the need to clarify the basis for choosing a candidate for delegation

There will be instances where delegation seems a much less complex thought process—for example, if you need flyers distributed around the office, choosing who can physically perform the task and is available. However, for employees with time management issues, this may not be an ideal quick job, as it can be drawn out exponentially. What seems like a simple task can be complicated based upon personal work ethic or background—this consistently falls back to the necessity of communication and a measurable deadline. When that employee with time management issues is available and physically capable, don't balk from utilizing them, but set a time constraint. This creates a concrete expectation, while can be evaluated. If the employee still exhibits behavior outside of the terms you explained, it's time to ask questions as part of your assessment process. This follow-up step will be treated later; at this point, focus on the fact that the third piece of successful delegation will be *communicating expectations*. Especially with delegation to subordinates, you are accountable for results.

Consequently, the best way to ensure results you are satisfied with is to provide clear direction. In more creative assignments, this is key as there is a broader scope of potential outcomes. For instance, if you ask an employee to create a newsletter for the group, communicate the topics to be highlighted, expectations on font (is this more professional or casual?), your directive on images (should they be included, is clip art acceptable, should they not be included to save ink?), will this be printed (and if so in color or black and white?), as well as an expected timeframe to have a draft completed. This may seem like an extensive and almost restrictive list of directions, but it actually only filters certain options to optimize a finished product in line with expectations. The actual content is still to be chosen by the delegate, with filters that you would choose if you completed the assignment yourself. If the assignment is more relaxed in expectation, less guidance is needed, so in addition to choosing the correct employee, ensure that your direction is proportionate to the specificity of the assignment. This decreases stress on the employee in trying to decode expectations, and allows enough creative freedom from the delegated task to be in part owned by he or she, increasing confidence and sense of self-efficacy.

As a leader, there are stages of delegation, the most basic of which is assessing what you need to get done. Next will come who is the appropriate person. Initially this is determined based upon skill set, but at an even deeper stage, you will come to evaluate not only skill set, but the needs of your team. With the right task, employee, and discussion of expectation, delegation is a symbiotic process. The same can be said for instances where you may delegate to a peer. In theory, this may seem like a foreign concept, but more than likely it is a practice used on a regular basis. One main difference is the level of communication needed, or the level of directive given. This interaction will typically be less formal and mandated, because of parallel entitlement levels. Within a team of managers, as with a team of agents, there are a variety of skill sets. A manager promoted from within may possess strong knowledge of processes and procedures, while a manager hired in at that level may be stronger in leadership or managerial skills. Another team member may be exceptional with technical issues and software. In this instance, the basic precept remains from delegating to employees—you have to know the skills on your team. At the management level, everyone should be able to complete most of the same tasks, but there will be definitive strengths that suggest each person for specific tasks. In informal settings, you may ask a manager to assist with a technical issue, which is in truth delegation as you are reassigning that task. However, this represents the team mindset among professionals, whereby you work as a supportive group. It's still important to attempt to leverage your employees first for simple technical issues, as the time commitment is less impactful at the agent level, but for complex issues above the agent's expertise, that peer is a fast resource to resolve the problem faster than you might be able to.

The situation may change if you are, in fact, that tech-savvy manager. If your time is being sapped by the same computer issue, for instance, evaluate the number of instances. Three agents needing help might take fifteen minutes of your time, but if the situation occurs and ends up taking an hour out of your day, delegate back to your peers. This can be as simple as quickly writing some instructions and dropping them off to each manager, explaining the steps to troubleshoot, but the onus is then placed on each manager to assist his or her team; alternatively, they can give the information to an agent and have them act as focal for technical issues. The infrequent call to help with a technical issue is the nature of having computer skills, but unless you work in technical support, this should not be a major part of your day. Gauge the time commitment, and if the problem goes beyond a simple fix, utilize that group. Your peers may resolve a quick issue faster than it would take IT, but beyond those situations, consider that their time is as valuable as yours and utilize the professionals whose occupation it is to resolve these issues.

It may seem counter-intuitive to delegate to a peer, since we assume they have a similar workload. In terms of people-management duties, this should be the case, unless they have a notably smaller team. Typically the distinction between commitments comes into play during projects. You might happen to be the employee who is seen as a skeleton key—you can fit pretty much anywhere and provide excellent results. While this is excellent for your year-end review, it can drastically increase your workload, often disproportionately to your peers. Know your limits; we are all human and admitting when you need help shows humility and wisdom, not to mention your dedication to results. In addition, take stock of the projects your peers own—is one clearly light on extra tasks? Present that to your manager and indicate that while you enjoy projects, you are currently overextended and thought a good solution would be to bring in your peer who currently has less tasks. Don't be a tattle-tale and complain that so-and-so has less to do. Use this opportunity to promote teamwork within your organization. Depending on the project duration and project details this may not be necessary, but chances are if you need relief from a task at a peer level, it's a recurring task that will require management approval to change hands.

You may be thinking it's not good to admit you are overextended— that would be the opposite of true. Understanding your limits and acknowledging that you are stretched thin before it affects your work displays leadership, reflection, and self-awareness. Bringing a solution along with that quandary is also a distinctly important part of the equation. Most people identify being busy at work, while few present a solution. Your boss will appreciate not only the honesty but also having some of the legwork done ahead of time. Assuming that you are given the go-ahead, there will likely be a conversation with yourself, your peer, and your boss. Is that still delegation, then? Yes. You initiated the change, requested the reallocation of duties. Regardless of who drives the conversation, you owned the choice to ask for this to happen. With simpler tasks, you can ask your peer to handle the occasional technical issue, but for long term projects affecting workload, the communication needs to be supported and often delivered by senior management. Your manager will still know that you exhibited the leadership to catalyze this change. Now, let's take off our rose-colored glasses for a moment, and acknowledge that your suggestion may not always get the go-ahead. Worry not, as that will be addressed. For now, let's focus on kudos for acknowledging our limits and seeking solutions.

Okay, enough celebrating. Last, but by no means least, is probably the least considered and conceptually most challenging type of delegation: managing up. While it may sound very intimidating, in truth, it shouldn't be. When there is a need, certain guidelines will offer assurance that delegating to your boss is the appropriate course. While there is a difference in authority, you are part of the same team, so there will be times when your manager needs to own certain tasks on which you should not work.

One example of such an instance involves you managing your peers. Unless your manager is on leave and you are a formal temporary replacement, formal performance reviews of your peers or disciplinary action should remain firmly with senior management. If you are tasked with those types of items, it can be uncomfortable to decline, but if you are given tasks involving personal information, that's an integrity issue. In the same way that you should not delegate tasks with employee information to that employee's peer, your manager should not place you in a similar situation. It can be a fine line between mentoring a peer and stepping into a managerial role, so consider the guidelines for delegating people tasks to your own employees. If you are coaching your peer, that is a "how" conversation, focusing on skill set and process. Conversations around behaviors or the "what" need to come from a level of authority that is lacking in peer to peer interactions. For example, if your manager asks you to clarify the time off policy at work with a new manager, you are simply providing facts or the process. If a manager asks you to talk to an employee about not following the time off policy, that is a behavior (i.e., what the employee does with time off) and should be a management conversation.

Another way to rationalize the difference is to consider the implications of the conversation. Explaining a system or expectation is re-stating what has already been approved by the company; it sets the parameters for acceptable behavior. Discussing whether performance meets or does not meet those standards can lead to disciplinary action. Additionally, the employee may explain certain extenuating circumstances to a manager that a peer does not need to know and is not entitled to know.

With some clarity on what should be maintained by your manager, the obvious question is—how to express that this task should be delegated to the manager? Adhere to the facts of the situation. For example:

> "Based upon the fact that employee benefit time is not information available to anyone other than the employee and his or her manager, it would infringe upon that privacy for me to get the details to give feedback. Also, if the use of benefit time should lead to disciplinary action, it's important that the

conversations leading to that decision are had with senior management, rather than a peer. I really appreciate having your esteem to handle the task, but based upon the topic and it being my peer I'm not the best option. Do you agree with that assessment?"

Most senior managers should recognize the implications as stated here and consent. If there is any disagreement, ask your manager to clarify the dissenting logic. Should you still feel that there is an ethical concern, there should be an ethics committee or even human resources outlet for you to utilize. You can even ask the question hypothetically to another senior manager that you trust; ultimately, if you feel moved to decline the task in the first place, it is likely a valid concern that your manager should respect.

Outside of tasks that are ethically questionable, there are additional projects that may simply lack the information to complete. In this case, the delegation to your manager will involve clarifying the scope of the project, the desired outcome, and how much latitude you have in design. You could be asked to create a brochure about the company you work for. How many different outcomes could that direction lead to? The first step is to be proactive—don't guess what is right and then get less than stellar feedback when you turn in the finished product. Similar to the parameters we discussed giving your employees, list questions to help narrow the scope of the task you are given, and pose these to your manager. Is this brochure for internal or external clients? That will guide if you can use jargon or layman's terms. Will this be disseminated electronically, in print, or both? This makes a difference in terms of font and layout. Can we print in color, or will this be in black and white? Should we give a broad overview of services, the company history, or client-facing employees? Is this brochure informational or designed to drive sales? Delegating back to your manager still leaves the task on your plate, but with a much clearer objective. You have essentially performed the delegation that should have happened when the task was assigned. Delegation is more commonly thought of as clearing an item off your plate for good, but even just having small pieces cared for can provide enormous relief. If you are operating under a less than clear idea of the scope, simply pushing that accountability back is delegating legwork and ensuring your success in the long term.

As an outstanding performer, your boss could also make you accountable for tracking your peer group's completion of mandatory tasks, for example, completing employee performance evaluations. While this is likely logged into an online tracking system and is not technically secure information, truly your manager should be the one to own this task. If you are simply reporting the data, that is just providing factual information. Consider suggesting that this report be sent to the entire management team, including your peers, to provide a status report. Should your manager then ask you to complete the status reports, this should be re-delegated back to your manager, simply because it is in the realm of his or her specific job duties.

It cannot be underestimated how imperative clear communication is to successful delegation. In instances where you delegate to an employee and are still accountable for the outcome, choosing the right person, setting clear expectations, and making a measurable deadline offers the best chance for a product you are proud of. Discretion proves equally important when discerning what tasks are appropriate to delegate to peers, especially assignments requiring a longer time commitment. Ultimately, perhaps the least discussed and most complicated is still delegating up. Communication of reasons for delegating up ensures that it is not perceived as shirking responsibility but rather as a keen assessment of the implications of a task. Whether managing up, down, or laterally, keep focused on the facts:

1. Who is the right choice for the task?

2. What is the desired outcome?

3. When should this be completed by?

Depending upon who you delegate to, there may be more creative freedom, but in considering these three basic concepts, you create a template for successful delegation that will make that decision simpler.

DELEGATION AND COMMUNICATION

"The two words information *and* communication *are often used interchangeably, but they signify quite different things. Information is giving out; communication is getting through."*

- Sydney Harris

I would highly recommend that you prepare a little sign for your office. It doesn't have to be hung on the wall for everybody to see. It doesn't have to be published in the organization's newsletter. It is a message for you and you alone:

GOOD DELEGATION REQUIRES GOOD COMMUNICATION

Get used to it. The "Jump!" "How high, sir?" mentality works only in the military, where there is at least the perception that the superior fully controls the life of the subordinate.

Nor is it acceptable to suppose that the delegate "really oughta wanta" do what he should. How often do you suppose that a teacher, faced with a student's failure, has said, "Well, I taught it; he should have learned it."

The truth of the communications morass is that for delegation to be successful, the delegate must "buy in" to the tasks for which he or she has been delegated. In today's parlance, we identify it as "getting with the program."

It isn't enough merely to spout words and assume the completion of one or more tasks. We could do that with SOPs (Standard Operating Procedures), and then we would discover that nobody reads the SOPs anyway. About the only way to overcome that mindset is to establish somebody's responsibility to "bird dog" the communications process— to see that Communicator A and Communicator B (C, D, and E) are "on the same page." The problem with that is that eventually the process is ignored.

We can successfully generate the dictum. We can make rules day in and day out. Having rules and people who understand them and are willing to follow them, might be sufficient in a world where no judgment is required. Realistically, then, what you want—and let's face it, you may have to train for it—is to provide the inputs, accept the outputs, and trust in the process that lies between. That's what delegation is. Not only must I advance the responsibility for a process or a project, I must provide the resources to operate that process or project, and I must trust the delegate to combine the two into a desired output that meets the vision of the delegator and the organization for whom both work.

So it follows that there are some communications techniques to consider. Important point: there is nothing special about the techniques of communication. What you will read here may also appear in a hundred other venues. What we desire for this treatise is some treatment of the subject from the perspective of delegation.

Organization

Consider organizing to facilitate communication. That's a mouthful with a very simple message: ensure that everybody on the affected communication plane knows what the goal is, how it is to be achieved, how its success may be measured. Sounds good, doesn't it? Why, then, is it so difficult to achieve?

Planning for communication in your organization is important, just as listing all the tasks that must be accomplished. Therefore, it begins with the delegator, who needs these data:

What has to be done? The delegator must be able to describe the product or result of the task being delegated. Included here would be a full knowledge of item specifications, levels of detail, deadlines, budgets, and how (and by whom) the resulting product or service will be used. The rationale for this is that everybody, from top to bottom, must have a concrete picture of the product and its working. We're after the "I didn't mean that" and the "that's not what I thought I was getting." One must fall back on the blind men, each having hold of a different part of an elephant analogy. From the delegation point of view, perhaps it would be wise to require all people to verbalize, preferably by writing it down, what their perception is of the project or process.

Who should do the work, i.e., be the delegate? Who has the skill, knowledge, and experience? Should that all be in one person? If yours is an organization of superstars, perhaps. The reality is that most organizations have a paltry number of people who have the entirety of skill, knowledge, and experience. If they do, they're looking for another job with higher pay. You would be wise to distribute the skills, the experience, and the knowledge among the work group, for another of your responsibilities is the farm team. You wish to assist the learning, development, growth, and engagement of everybody on your team. If you do not do those things, those people will go to where those considerations as given. Does that sound pessimistic? Any manager who is not building his own team while working on the organization's projects is asking to be replaced. It's that important.

Select the delegate and identify what training and coaching will be necessary. Begin your project by matching the tasks or activities to the most suitable person. Use this data to assist your determination: What time will be required to "get up to speed?" What training or coaching will this person require? What are your practices relative to skills and strengths and your interests in career development? And what is this individual's current workload?

Advance Delegation

Theoretically, this process called delegation is not a daily activity as pertains to one manager and one delegate, so long as the plan is fixed and both parties have accepted its rationale. Therefore, it follows that the delegation that is done is largely done in advance of the assignment of the task or process. The concept of "effective communication" is straightforward. Enter those two words into Google and you'll find some good instruction, along these lines:

- The skill of active listening.
- The skill of asking questions that helps both parties reach a common understanding.
- The skill of verbal (oral) communication to articulate the message to minimize misunderstandings.
- The skill of using and responding to nonverbal communication appropriately. There's a 25 cent word for this—kinesics (body language).
- The skills of paraphrasing and summarizing to clarify

understanding and ensure both parties agree as to what has been discussed.

In this book, we will not focus on listening skills, interpretation of nonverbal gestures, or in the negotiation processes whereby an agreement is reached. There are many options for that study.

What Are The Choices?

There are a few to consider, none of which is particularly strange. They boil down to two, each with a set of facilities, a set of constraints, a set of positives, and a set of negatives.

Directives: These are the written documents. They aren't necessarily procedures, though their contents may be procedural. These are the job statements, resource allocations, staff identifications, promises made, promises elicited, obligations made, obligations accepted, feedback, and reporting items, most often generated downward in the organization. From a delegation perspective, what is written must be those elements of record, those things that may be provided against the oral specifications initially given, such that they document everybody's understanding.

Meetings: These are the data verification and information dissemination steps, the progress reporting, the problem resolution, and the trouble-shooting or "tweaking" activities done in a face-to-face method. Nothing is done here that couldn't be done with correspondence, and yet the meeting is a blanket dissemination that is heard by all participants at the same time, allowing full understanding—and immediate feedback—between management and participants.

As a project progresses well, meetings are great "attaboy" sessions, building morale, identifying surface problems that are ripe for easy resolution. In fact, some will hold that such meetings are superfluous. However, as a project progresses poorly, they become very much a "gripe" session, the source of organizational black humor, and frequently the scene of a search for the guilty and the promotion on the noninvolved. From a delegation perspective, tasks lists should be developed pursuant to a meeting, the commitment of the people should be secured, and the agreements archived.

There are several kinds of meetings:

The formal meeting—the "dog and pony show," where a summary of observations, the most important findings, the requests for resources, and the presentation of options for consideration or delivery are accomplished. This is an important meeting because the hierarchy—those empowered to commit resources—must be appraised of the high points without becoming involved in the minutiae of the detail. Think "Executive Summary."

The informal meeting—the "meeting of the minds," generally by the middle management staff in places ranging from the water cooler to the scheduled conference room. Often these meetings deal with isolated problems—problems that may not be of interest to the entire project or process team. More often than not, there will be no record of such meetings.

Progress meeting—these meetings will often be scheduled on a regular basis, such as each Monday morning. Here the persons responsible for a specific set of tasks will meet to work out interfaces, track task accomplishment, revise plans, request additional resources, identify roadblocks that must be removed by authority figures, and to chronicle the forward progress in terms of the steps accomplished per resources utilized. Minutes are normally kept for such meeting, and those minutes become a reading file available to anyone in the organization with an interest in tracking the process or project.

Harvey Gollub, previously mentioned former head of American Express, in his project laws postulated this one: "Project members despise project reporting because it so vividly demonstrates their lack of progress. Yours will be no different."

That may be true for one specific reason: very often, the progress report highlights a difficulty that should have been identified in the planning process. The problem isn't that the team should stop everything and wait for the re-planning to be done. Unfortunately, that isn't an available luxury. We are IN the plan that was devised. We have discovered an ERROR or OMISSION from the plan that was devised. And we must overcome the deficiency "on the fly," often requiring revisions to the plan—at least in the mind of the people paying the price— *without changing the delivery date.*

The italicized words are important and are often the source of downward pressure upon the project or process team. In fact, there is pressure all along the line to meet what some project members feel are unreasonable constraints in the first place. Crank in a problem or two and the emotional pressure placed upon the team, and that team will become convinced that honesty is not the best policy. It becomes worse. Punish the team members for being accurate and honest and find that their preference of one post-project "dressing down" is preferable to several conducted along the line.

It's at this point where the black humor begins to appear: "We the unwilling, led by the unqualified, doing the unnecessary and often the unthinkable, and working for the ungrateful" signs may, in some form, appear in any organization. Often they are augmented by signs that state, "We have done the impossible without resources for so long it is now possible for us to do everything with nothing." If this happens, this is what you will hear:

- It's more important to assign blame than it is to solve the problem.

- It's important to protect my fiefdom, perquisites, and privileges. If the problem is identified, you'll find out it wasn't in my area of responsibility.

- It's easier to talk sports than it is to focus on bottlenecks and improvements.

- It seems that this is the time when we declare that we are overworked and/or underpaid.

- It's not my fault. If !@#$% MANAGEMENT would just get its act together and do _____, we wouldn't have this problem at all.

- Meetings can devolve into who's happy, who is not, why certain people are problematic, or, "the rumor is that...."

- Often it's a search for the guilty and punishment for the innocent. Worse, occasionally it's the attack on the innocent and promotion of the guilty.

If that isn't enough, the process becomes iterative—it goes back to the top of the list and begins again with the finger pointing and accusations. It's no wonder that employees feel it is just the same crap, different day.

Go into any meeting and you will see a handful of speakers and a bucketful of mutes. The speakers are normally the outgoing individuals in the organization and because they are such, they often steer discussions, conclusions, and their following actions, more so on the action of their personalities rather than the situation of their positions. The mutes may be the "go alongs to get along," but they are the first to claim that the results may not be to their liking, creating an undercurrent that tells you that you'll be meeting again on this topic.

In any meeting, people are like icebergs. What you see in an individual represents only 10 percent of what's there. The remaining 90 percent is hidden. If it is important to elicit their response, then it is the responsibility of the moderator to open that portion of a meeting attendee's psyche.

Why Progress Communication Is Important

To begin with, this seems like it should be obvious. A project or a process has a defined schedule and a defined set of tasks. The people who are funding the project or process have a right to know how it is going.

- Are the tasks that should be done by this time completed?
- Have the expenditures that were purposed for this project or process matched the schedule?
- Has the assessment of available benefits change significantly? Positive? Negative?
- Has the environment that caused this project or process to be undertaken changed in a manner that might remove or change the need?
- Have there been major roadblocks and if so, have there been problems in getting them solved?
- Are we still on track for the expenditure of resources envisioned?
- Are we still on track for the flow of benefits to begin?

- If we are not, why not and what must be done to get the process back on track?

Depending on the size, complexity, experience, and length of the task/activity delegated, you will need to have progress update meetings on a somewhat regular schedule. These ensure that the task is moving in the right direction, that they are on the right track and to make changes at appropriate stages before it is too late, e.g. when the delegates think that they have completed the task. Here are some guidelines:

Schedule your progress update meetings and stick to the schedule. Predictability is important.

Outline the minimum requirements for every meeting in terms of "planned versus actual." Recognize that often, tasks that are ahead of schedule may provide resources for those that are behind schedule. Knowing their statuses when they occur provides the capability to adjust.

As with any meeting, there should be a leader. Organizationally the tendency is an "us versus them" mentality, where the person in the hierarchy assumes control. If you do that, don't be surprised that the project or process team feels "under fire." Many organizations have had great success with designating a rotating moderator for the meeting. To begin with, this ensures participation by all the people involved. Carrying forward, that moderator may make assignments for meeting contributions from other team members.

The same communications skills are applicable to meetings—active listening, open discussion—controlled, to be sure—and an atmosphere where people feel comfortable to air the problems they either cannot resolve themselves or which require temporary extra-team participation.

It is human nature to want to "dump" the responsibility of a problem area. If you have created an atmosphere where concerns or difficulties may be expressed, you have a responsibility to listen, yes, but your responsibility also includes the need to have everybody in the room to understand. In some cases, you may recognize that the person raising the issue simply cannot do some task—probably for reasons of time or skill—and the team must then find ways to obtain time or skill. Nevertheless, most importantly, the team must continue to hold the person who raised the issue responsible for its resolution. Taking the task away merely proves to the individual that he or she may gain credit for its accomplishment without having to produce the results that led to the accomplishment. To that end, the first practice is to seek the insight of the person responsible for the task. Chances are he or she has a solution. The purpose of the progress meeting is to encourage that person to offer and then implement that solution, unless other members have experience that emphatically denies the action.

In 1974, writing in the Harvard Business Review, William Oncken and Donald Wass wrote *Management Time: Who's Got the Monkey?* Enter the italicized words into Google and you will see that the article has been updated by the likes of Steven Covey (Seven Secrets) and Kenneth Blanchard (One Minute Manager). You can read about it at: http://www.hfrr.ksu.edu/doc2361.ashx and other places. The jewel from that article is this: "How managers can avoid becoming walking lint collectors for their subordinates' problems."

So don't take over the problem. Lead the subordinates to resolve any problems themselves, especially if the solutions lie within their organizational strata. Good management—the delegators—should agree on and provide the support needed. Remember, at this point, it is insufficient to tell a project group that they "must do" with the allocated resources and within the time originally allocated before any problems were detected. Constructive feedback falls next, but must always be inviting rather than directive in nature.

Patience may be a virtue, but it's necessary when it comes to project progress meetings. It is very easy to pontificate, announcing that you could do the work in some abbreviated time. Recognize that the function of a manager is to help work to be accomplished through others. If your future is to be upward in your organization, then you must learn of your responsibility to develop your team.

There's a name for that—it's called *empowerment*. If the subordinate feels that he or she simply cannot complete (or even keep up with) the task, then agreeing to deal with it removes the responsibility from the team. You don't want that. This now means that not only the assignment must be delivered lower in the hierarchy, but the authority to meet and conquer any problems must be included, as well—including the resources to do so. In such a manner, the communication is clear, timely, thorough, and honest. In turn, the responsible team members receive the "bennies" of good motivation, reverence, and reward.

Don't overlook the fact that the progress report meeting is a place where kudos for good performance should be given, but at the same time, remember that the kudos must be applied to the team, not to individuals on the team. While it may seem beneficial at first, the designation of MVP one week might lead to the status of the "bum of the week" the next. The project must rise and fall on the basis of the team. When the project is done, there are many ways to reward outstanding performance, even of individuals. Nevertheless, during the period of the project or process, all team members are equal—all have responsibility for accomplishment—and all must participate in both rewards and constraints.

Specific Communication Needs of the Delegation Process

- During the analysis of need: If we can accept the premise that you must delegate because you cannot simply do everything yourself, it follows that the ability to develop a team is based on the resource allocations. Most organizations of size keep time sheets of some sort. Assuming that it isn't punishing to tell the truth, the time sheets for management should show where the time is being spent, for it is from the time already spent that a determination can be made as to whether an additional, new, or revised project can be undertaken. The same is true for every potential member of the team. The communication of the numbers should be the sole determinant of the availability of time resources. If it is not, then either the time sheets do not convey an accurate representation of how time is spent or somebody is telling his boss what he or she wants to hear.

- During the evaluation of options: It's called a production possibilities curve. Remove the resource from one task and apply it to another and you change the critical nature of each task. That tradeoff must be documented. Further, the decision must be made as to the relative worth of each of the options being considered, for after all, the job involves far more than two options. The situation is never an "either/or" selection. More often than not, it's a "this and this and that" scenario. Delegation, then, depends on the pressure points in the evaluation of tradeoffs. The addition of a new task will, of necessity, affect—and be affected by—other commitments previously made. Now the communication becomes a little more dicey, for you at one time made a commitment to Interested Party A. Along came Interested Party B and if you accept—and commit to—a priority from B, it must, by definition, affect Interested Party A. Should not party A have an input on the new project or process under consideration?

- If the most effective delegation system is one that you can trust and will grow and change as your needs grow and change, then among your options must be hiring, training, outsourcing, or contracting some work (not necessarily the new work) to others. If the choice is between a new hire and an external contractor, there is a host of other problems to be considered, and many of them are communications-based. An external consultant or contractor brings another insight for communication—that individual or group of individuals are totally divorced from the organization structure, and the only leverage then lies with the project or process itself. For that reason, their participation in internal meetings and written progress reporting become paramount.

- Write it down: From the inception of the idea to the final report, document everything. Write memos of invitation. Write memos of understanding. File statements of concurrence. Create a troubleshooting file of problems for which some team member has a declared responsibility. Keep a file of project completions. Certainly keep files of progress reports. Ensure that documents that must be read by everybody are initialed by the readers before they are filed. This process is a challenge, not only because it takes time to do, but also is prima facie evidence of what is not yet complete, is presenting insurmountable obstacles, and further demonstrates the possibility that the plans, and by definition the planners, were insufficient. Here's a new sign:

YOU CAN'T DELEGATE WHAT YOU DON'T DOCUMENT

- Summarize; summarize: All of the processes and systems that are involved in this project or process must themselves be documented. It matters not that the methods used have been there since the inception of the organization. The project or process being developed must interface with the systems and process that exist. Complete documentation of what exists and how this project or process interfaces will allow any team member with suitable skills to refocus on areas that are lacking or where a replacement must be scheduled. These documents must be centrally located and available at least to middle management individuals at any time during the course of the project.

- Prioritize Your Options: The theory, at least, is that you align the task to be done with the person skilled to do it. People who study such things assert that if the task lists are not prioritized, over a very short period, everything will be equally critical. When things become equally critical, nobody knows what to do first, and the net result is that the reports of progress become reports of doldrums—and thus, the Harvey Gollub quotation that began this chapter.

- Use the tools: the latest tools of technology can provide a "leg up" on the communications process. Message boards for the project provide up-to-date listings of problems, successes, and accomplishments. Properly structured and with the use of graphic presentation, project members and other interested parties can monitor the project or process from the information tablet. Virtual meetings via Skype or other software, such as www.gotomeeting.com, provide the capabilities to interact with project members next door or around the world in real time. Working together in a room is one option, of course, but collaborators may come from several different disciplines whose time and skill are utilized only as necessary. The tools permit their inclusion when they are needed and their release when their contribution is used. Online communication provides many other benefits. Message boards and forums allow people who are not a part of the project or process to contribute suggestions, ideas, and experiences that may be applied to the problem(s) at hand. These contributions may be direct (do this), indirective (look here), or inductive (have you considered). Often the smallest tidbit of experience will launch a research effort that results in a solution to the problem or a break in the logjam of delay.

- Communicate Often: Without communication, you have no team. Without concise communication, people will not participate in the communication process. In Shakespeare's Hamlet, Act 2, Scene 2, the bard says: "Brevity is the soul of wit." How often do we hear "Let's cut to the chase," or "Get to the point." Years ago, a TV detective said, "Just the facts, ma'am." So communicate the essentials and put the nonessentials in a reading file. Just make sure that all the information is available to all the involved and/or interested parties.

- Trust is a two-way street. When a project or a process is delegated to a subordinate or to a team, the higher level must be able to trust what is being told and reported by the team. They must trust it implicitly, and, for safety's sake, they must document and test the trust. The team, on the other hand, must trust that when a problem becomes known, particularly one that requires extra-project resolution, that it will be done, promptly, completely, and thoroughly. That seems like a reasonable set of requests, but more than once a manager has conveyed that trust in words not dissimilar to "What did you do with all the resources that I promised you?" More than once a team has told the project manager and even a member from higher in the organization what he or she wanted to hear. Once it starts either way, chaos results. The easiest example of this is the depiction of Mickey Mouse functioning to the Dukas composition *The Sorcerer's Apprentice* in the animated musical *Fantasia*.

To summarize: We wish to use communication as a vehicle to collaborate, share information, build our team, accomplish our goals, and make an indelible contribution to the forward progress of our organization. Whether formal or informal, the door must be open and the process must be interactive. Building trust is a key issue. Building confidence that communicating the information—all of it—when pertinent is important. Building the assurance that the team generates the information and the team is affected by the information generated will not assure that all projects will be completed on time. What it does is to assure people that they are free to share problems, offer suggestions, and gather information from all affected levels, top to bottom, and there will be nothing but praise and encouragement for doing so.

With a View Toward The Future

Delegation implies many people, the dissemination of information to those people, and the gathering of data from among them as the basis for making organization decisions.

That's great for existing organizations in situ (in the original place). Organizations with a history have long-since given up the individual entrepreneur form of organization in exchange for the division of responsibilities model. However, just as you can take the boy out of his habitat but cannot take the habitat out of the boy, there is a natural reluctance--or perhaps an abject disdain—of doing those "team things." How many businesses began because one person with an entrepreneurial spirit took the mantle of organization on his own shoulders, only to discover that he or she was faced with the recognition that the organization is too small to acquire people to do all those tasks, but too large for one person to do everything.

Nevertheless, they go into business for themselves anyway. They may be loners. They may eschew structure. They may have a low tolerance for nonsense. Therefore, they choose to start a business rather than face a seemingly impossible phalanx of people to rise to management level or even salaried positions. They want to do the work, not talk about it. They don't want to have to worry about building an organization. Their reward is in the innovation, the risk taking, and their direct control of their unique destinies. They derive no "fun" if they must hire people, instruct them, and manage their progress. After a while, however, they awaken to a very simple fact—there is a maximum growth potential that they will never be able to exceed if they insist on doing everything themselves.

You need not go far to recognize this. Pick a few names: Bill Gates, Steve Jobs, Mark Zuckerberg, Bill Hewlett, David Packard, Michael Dell, Gordon Moore, Elon Musk, and Richard Branson. Each of these people had to "get over" the idea that they couldn't do everything themselves. Each has learned to delegate and the successes they have achieved bear record of how well they have done so.

Developing a team isn't difficult, if you'll apply some fundamental principles and strategies. If you are careful to set it up so they leverage you, then you are headed for success. You feel supported. They feel success for the participation. It happens because of a simple maxim:

I AM RESPONSIBLE FOR MORE WORK THAN I CAN PERFORM

Another sign, perhaps. But making that transition isn't easy, and the result has been the emergence of the business coach, whose out-of-house objectivity often becomes the leverage that makes the entrepreneur aware that if he is to grow, then he must—to use President Reagan's words—"trust but verify." That takes communication.

Communication through delegation builds teamwork and teaches the use of others' power. When those efforts are done incorrectly, it's a waste of money not only for the principals but for the organization itself. Put that communication into a program of shaping people into the people you need to effectively and efficiently run the organization, and watch the difference. You can teach people to be competent, operating by the numbers. That may get the work done. Or you can help them not only learn competency but strive for perfection. That happens when you communicate the job which is assigned, the place where the work fits within the organization, and the benefit to all the parties that emerges from the employee's participation.

But Communication Isn't Easy

It certainly is not. To begin with, you must separate the position from the human that occupies it. Large organizations tend to revere the position more than the human. To many, we're seen as cogs in a huge wheel. That's perhaps wise for the Board of Directors down to and including the Second Vice President. In the trenches, however, it has to change. The interaction is now face-to-face and well endowed with kinesics.

The new entrepreneur does have a unique opportunity, however. He or she can create something radically different and far more effective. New communications methods, supported by ever-evolving communications vehicles, allow all levels of a project, from upper-level management all the way down into the trenches to have the most current up-to-date decision criteria. Those are the numbers—perhaps presented graphically—that will dictate action, or if no action, provide progress signals.

Teamwork gives you other options, as well. Not only are your strengths exploited, you now have access to others with similar—or supportive—talents and like-minded passions about the work to be done and the benefit to the organization itself. If the correct word—if the correct encouragement—if the correct taking of the pulse of the people in your team is done, then you have opened a fountain for the free flow of creativity. This creativity will lead to accelerated task accomplishments and the satisfaction of a job well done. This, in turn, launches subsequent phases on a high level of personal satisfaction.

ANY JOB WORTH DOING IS WORTH DOING WELL

This will now allow you to focus on and tap into everybody's talents in a way that channels them toward the completion of their tasks, the team's assignment, and the organization's benefits. It does something else, as well. It leads to praise, to additional self-motivation, and to more deeply concentrated efforts.

Communication is always a two-way street. In order for communication to happen, not only must the message be sent, but it also must be received. Some of your best ideas may not happen simply because you don't share them in a way that others can understand. Things that may seem obvious to you may not be so obvious to your team members, who are coming from a different perspective and don't share your stake in the business.

Recognize also that no two people communicate in precisely the same manner. In order for team members to communicate, they must be "on the same page." This means that both parties must go out of their way to ensure a mutual understanding of the words, pictures, and nuances in any project or process situation. It is so easy to miscommunicate. English is a much-nuanced language. Often the image of a communication is entirely different on the part of the receiver from the intent of the sender. Whenever and wherever there are differences in geography, culture, non-native language, or interpretation, there are areas where the communication process can bog down or take an entirely new and unintended direction. The danger is that we question competence when we ought instead to question understanding.

The mental obstacles of delegation communication are many. If a supervisor is reviewing a task with a subordinate, the superior's perception may be to verify that all the appropriate steps have been taken. The subordinate's position may be, "Doesn't he think I know how to do my job?" Any team member who feels cheated in any manner may well react negatively. There are companies that make different delegations to different job levels, for example. The position of the office is, of course, a perquisite for organizational management. But some firms go further, detailing the size of tile on the floor, the allocation of wood versus metal desks, the decorations on the wall—even the curtains on the window. Communication doesn't have to be merely audible or readable words and pictures. To quote Robert Townsend's book, *Up The Organization*, "The premier parking space should go to the first person to arrive at work."

Then there is the communication of fear. "Get it done or I'll have to do it myself." Not very motivating for a subordinate team looking to please the boss and affect the organizational environment. Often a manager will hold off on a project in anticipation that the "perfect" worker will appear—one who can do the job with little or no direction. It doesn't happen. All that happens is that the work gets delayed until there is no option other than giving it to somebody who might have made the deadline had he or she been allowed to start and to gather the skills and knowledge to do the work. Now, at the last moment, everything has become critical. Couple that with the difficulty of giving off any work that the top person considers is important to his or her personal career, and you can understand the reluctance to give control to anybody.

Summary

It's part and parcel of the process. Delegation hands out the tasks. Teamwork performs the work. Communication in all directions and in all modes is what makes it happen. You want the right people; you want them correctly placed; and you want a bi-directional communication process. If you will concentrate on building trust and opening up the avenues and methods of communication, your delegation will work, the project or process will be completed, and your team will develop—and maintain—a high degree of motivation, both individually and as a unit. The long-term benefit is increased competence, a "can do" attitude, and a record of satisfactory accomplishment.

WHEN NOT TO DELEGATE

"Leadership is the art of getting someone else to do something you want done because he wants to do it."

- Dwight D. Eisenhower

Now that there are principles in place for what to delegate, who to delegate to and how to communicate effectively, it's important to examine situations when you should not delegate. One of the easiest rules of delegation is the time needed to delegate versus the time it takes you to complete a task. As a general rule, if you can complete a task in less time than it takes to explain and delegate, perform the task yourself. For one reason, you are guaranteed a reliable outcome. Another benefit is that although this is an additional item on your checklist, the brief time to complete allows for a satisfying check mark when the item is done. This task could be as simple as pulling a status report, but while you are an expert in the system, training a new person to complete the task takes not only the time to explain but can likely lead to more questions, negating any time you would gain by not performing the task personally. In most cases, tasks falling under this rule should take five minutes or less—a time commitment easily met and not large enough to impact your plan for the day.

Communication is clearly an essential piece in the delegation process. One simple reason not to delegate is when the final objective or scope of an assignment or project is not clear. Without clear goals or targets, the ambiguous task that you as a leader can navigate may overwhelm your team and creates increased likelihood of poor results. Do your agents the courtesy of not delegating a task where you can't explain the ultimate goal or desired outcome. You are still responsible for the finished product when you delegate, so in nebulous situations, it's best to maintain ownership, at least until you gain further instructions on the true objective.

In a similar vein there will be some tasks that have a clear objective but are difficult to explain—weigh your list of obligations for the day. If you are over-extended, don't take the time to delegate a task you know you can complete faster than any potential delegates. When you have free time or are searching for developmental opportunities, this can be a time to delegate duties requiring more explanation. Until that opportunity arises, and it will, given your new-found delegation, organization and prioritization skills, be honest about the tasks that are simple checklist items you can handle. One instance might be requesting profile changes for employees within your organization's software program (think login access or security code/swipe cards). This can be a tedious job, comprised of requesting new profiles, changing profiles as team members change groups, and requesting the deletion of profiles for those no longer employed. Because of the multiple steps involved, the impact if not completed correctly, and your familiarity with the software and the level of interaction with management, it is a task not easily delegated. If you do not have time to explain these steps, complete the process in chunks, allowing yourself periods of time over multiple days. Be sure to create a checklist for each type of change request to ensure you do not miss any steps, as this can impact an employee's ability to work or create a security concern for terminated employees.

Additionally, you can have an honest conversation with your manager about the priority of this assignment. Let's assume that for the same task, you do not have any employees who can satisfactorily complete the task in your place, or your manager does not want this delegated. This is a likely situation, and may incite feelings of being stuck. Don't give in to that mindset, but evaluate your priorities against this task. Have a candid conversation with your manager about the duties you need to complete and where this falls in that list. If you agree about the priority of the assignment and the need to complete other tasks first, pushing back other deadlines may need to happen. If the timelines are not flexible, revisit your list of obligations. It may become necessary to prioritize and then delegate other tasks on your list. For a monthly project, this may mean you have an employee or peer temporarily step in, as may happen with the case of employee profile requests. This task cannot be put off, as it is necessary for agents to perform their job duties. However, if you own additional tasks with similar importance, they need to be reallocated to another. Because your manager is adamant that the profile requests cannot be delegated and you don't have sufficient time for another duty, you will have to make allowances elsewhere. Remember that although you should not delegate employee performance feedback to an agent, your peers can help with this in a pinch, even just by entering the feedback into your tracking system, while you still have the coaching conversation. Delegation is born out of necessity, because management roles often involve more work than can be completed in an expected timeframe. If the work cannot be delegated, we must then rely upon our understanding of what the most important aspects of the job description are in conjunction with senior management's prioritization of tasks.

In some cases, when you meet with your manager, he or she may explain that a task will take precedence over a project you and/or your team is currently working on; this could be a time-sensitive task, such as training your team on a new process prior to a huge system update or new product launch. Because of the time constraints and potential client impact, you as a leader must ensure your team has the correct information and knowledge to perform their jobs. This may mean setting aside monthly one-on-one progress meetings, but in the larger picture means your team avoids frustration when the process changes and they are unaware or untrained. Depending upon the change, it may fall to you to train this update because of your group's role; be sure that you have a clear objective of the key takeaways, create a handout highlighting those points, and take attendance to be sure each of your agents is included or later debriefed on the changes. Small preparation can help focus the training, eliminating wasted time and panic after the process update if questions were not answered. The same principle applies to most tasks—rather than diving in frantically, take a moment to assess and develop a course of action. This may prevent missed steps later on, redundancies in work, and eliminates the guesswork about which tasks remain.

While time-sensitive assignments may cause certain things like performance meetings to be delayed, tasks involving sensitive information about employees should truly not be delegated unless you are on extended leave. Typically, formal conversations take place on a routine basis (monthly, quarterly, yearly) and evaluate agent progress against previous metrics and improvement targets. It is important these conversations come from a place of authority as peers are not privy to performance statistics; this information should be maintained between agent and manager. Similar to the discussion of your manager not delegating peer performance feedback to you, this should also never be done to your team. The distinction lies, as we have stated, between providing the "what" and the "how". In a call center environment, for instance, anyone in the phones area can hear an agent on the phone who may struggle to explain a certain policy. A peer can coach the "how" on this policy by suggesting another talk-off that they learned from experience. This type of informal coaching is a suggestion or tool, not in any way correlated to performance statistics or private information.

Alternatively, in a call center the same agent may be monitored and heard giving misinformation, which would result in adverse action, such as a failed call for wrong information. In this instance, the agent provided incorrect data (the "what"), and it impacted performance ratings. This information needs to come from a designated place, namely, you as the manager. In addition to the authority you have to access and assess performance, you also have the professional experience to explain the noted defect and provide correct information in a diplomatic way.

It is key when employees repeatedly sustain poor performance that you personally have documented conversations around the expectation, the current performance, and the outcomes if the behavior does not change. As the manager, you are accountable for managing the whereabouts of your workforce, and taking disciplinary action if continued improvement does not occur. This should not be delegated to a peer, as he or she is not familiar with the employee and, it is important to take credit for your follow-through. Additionally, such information is absolutely sensitive and should involve only the absolute necessary individuals, be it your manager or human resources, based upon company policy. "Firing" employees is not a pleasant process, but as a leader, part of your role is to ensure that the team you manage performs to business standards and take action when they do not. Having hard conversations may necessitate having another party in the meeting, but as you have firsthand knowledge of the case, it is imperative that you be present. Delegation does not relieve leaders of the hard tasks, but merely affords them the time to complete those items to the best of their abilities.

In direct opposition to being part of employee termination are those tasks you are passionate about. This could be a process improvement that you conceptualized and have gained so much enthusiasm for that it spreads into your entire workday. As we've already stated—that is not a phenomenon to be taken lightly. When so many are downtrodden at their jobs, finding a project that evokes tenacity and passion in yourself benefits not only you, but anyone you interact with. Enthusiasm is contagious, and enthusiasm at work is so rare that it will set you apart. Considering the prioritization and organization you have already performed--likely you have found other tasks to delegate leaving free time for this project. It could be the creation of a timeline tracking business changes for an improvement committee. Taking time to be creative and develop the visual representation may be the piece you truly enjoy—hold onto that task and perhaps share the information gathering with peers or your team. If the opposite is true, and you are truly excited about all of the changes your business has made and explaining those, but the idea of creating the template is too tedious, hold on to whatever it is that incites that passion for the task. By breaking down the assignment, the time commitment is even more manageable—do not delegate away parts of your job that give you enjoyment. Once you find ways to sustain your happiness and engagement at work, you will find yourself more productive, and the effects of this become magnified in those around you.

Let's evaluate the opposite situation—you have what in your mind is a great assignment but the employee is clearly not enthusiastic about the task. Of course, it's important to probe and understand reasons for that hesitation, but ultimately if the lack of passion is there—don't delegate that task to that individual! Regardless of whether you or your agent complete the task, the responsibility falls into your lap for the outcome, so don't risk underwhelming results if there is a clear indicator of apathy for the assignment. The same holds true for difficult tasks or changes that you know will not be happily accepted—do not pawn those tasks off on someone else, or displace the responsibility of having those difficult conversations. Managing a team is a lot like marriage—for better or for worse, for richer or for poorer, you are invested in this partnership.

One additional instance where you should not delegate is an assignment that increases your visibility or has the potential to build more business relationships that can further your career goals. It sounds calculated, and truly as a leader, you should evaluate not only the task itself, the prioritization and microcosmic details, but how it may benefit you. Does this project involve senior officials you've not yet interacted with? That's an opportunity to display your skills and network. Perhaps this task requires you to apply your current knowledge for another group to update processes, and you are striving to get into that other project task group. Working with those individuals builds relationships that strengthen your application as a potential candidate in the future. All of this, of course, relies upon how you perform throughout the duration of the assignment, and the final outcome. Essentially, you need to be on top of your game. We've already covered that when you delegate to subordinates, you are accountable for their performance. In this situation, you are front and center to be evaluated. Don't be intimidated, and remember the long term benefits of projects of this nature when you prioritize tasks. It may relieve pressure to place these tasks higher on your to-do list, so that they can be completed with thoughtfulness (and, bonus, once completed, you can resume your typical work items without the looming pressure of a project that could determine your next career move). Keep in mind that while your role as a leader is to develop your people, it's essential not to forget your own professional trajectory.

In the end, it comes down to the delicate balancing act that quantifies leadership. You juggle not only routine assignments, long term projects, and your team, but must match which tasks and people provide the most successful outcome. There is no perfect formula, but keep in mind the following key considerations:

1. If you cannot explain the objective, it's not a good task to assign.

2. If it takes longer to provide instruction than to complete the task, there is no time-saving benefit. (Thus, if you are delegating

to save time, it's not a good option.)

3. If delegating a task creates more questions and follow-ups, it's not a time-saving task to delegate.

4. If your manager does not permit delegation of a task, that's a hard limit. Look for other tasks with changeable deadlines or the potential to be delegated, even temporarily.

5. If the content is sensitive, do not delegate.

6. If the conversation is a difficult one, this is not cause for delegation. The initiative to have hard conversations separates leaders from bosses.

7. If you are passionate about a task, hold onto it. Job satisfaction is never to be underrated.

8. If your employee is not up for the task, do not delegate. The final results are your responsibility, and who you delegate to is also noted, in conjunction with the outcome.

9. If an assignment allows for your career development, hold onto that assignment and give yourself the chance to shine!

TRACKING PROJECTS

"You cannot be effective if those who work for you are not. So building their effectiveness ought to be a priority."

- Richard N. Haass

For several chapters now we have talked about prioritizing tasks, breaking a project into smaller parts, and your accountability for results, even in a delegated situation. It's time to discuss how you manage those tasks, even after delegation. In most instances, this will involve delegating to a subordinate, although in some instances you may own a project and delegate specific tasks to your peers, which will require follow-up. The level of input and types of conversations will differ based upon your audience, so we will treat each separately. In addition, from a senior management level, delegating to general management still requires followup, which is of a different nature. First, let's examine the most common scenario—delegating to your agent-level team.

It's important to recognize that, as with all management decisions, balance is a necessity. Depending upon the temperament of your employee and his or her knowledge base, more or less involvement may be needed. However, for any projects delegated to your team, checkpoints are necessary. Each type of assignment will require evaluation of progress on your part. Let's take a rather basic and simple task—data entry. The assignment is deceptively simple and begs the question—why are checkpoints needed? Stay with me, here. The first piece of successful delegation, as we've discussed, is communication. Once you have selected your delegate, estimate the time needed to complete the task. Meet with your employee, explain the task and expected deadline, then ask for his or her input—does the timeframe seem fair? Make sure that you not only specify the number of hours it will require, but also if you want the task finished by a particular date, set that guideline. Be sure to pay careful attention to the recipient's bearing and signals—we have mentioned that the desire to help with the task is equally as important as the skill set involved.

Assuming that your employee is happy to assist, evaluate checkpoints within the assignment. For example, if the data entry is lengthy but should take no more than a day, designate your own halfway checkpoint, perhaps after lunch before the employee starts working. You should have explained that the task will most likely take one day and that you need it by the end of business, today. When you ask your employee to explain the status, have specific quantitative questions to evaluate progress. If you ask "how's that data entry coming?" and your employee says "I'm still working on it", you have determined that he or she is on task, but have no concept of the pace and whether the task is on track for completion by the end of the day. Obtaining key details to specifically evaluate performance will require minimal preparation on your part, but incites better results from your employees, as it creates detailed accountability. This may be as simple as number pages to be entered, designating which page is the halfway point, and asking your employee after lunch which page he or she is currently working on. Simple, right? So why does this never happen? There is a pervasive mentality that delegation is like daycare—drop off your child and that's one item off your to-do list. This may be fine in some cases, but consider the importance of direction and communication. At the end of the day, you are responsible for that child, the same as with a delegated task, and regardless of how great your team is, you are still responsible for managing them. I repeat, delegation is not the end of your involvement, especially when delegating to subordinates. Provide measurable deadlines to your team, but create measurable checkpoints and you will avoid failure to meet deadlines or sloppily completed projects.

Considering our example above, let's consider possible outcomes of using a measurable checkpoint. If page 50 is the midpoint, but your employee is on page 60, clearly he or she is ahead of the target. This does not mean the conversation should end with a generic "good." Acknowledge that he or she is ahead of midpoint, and ask that the pace be maintained. Quickly calculate the average pages entered per hour, and share with the agent that based upon this morning's performance, he or she completes 15 pages per hour, so the task should be completed roughly an hour before end of day. Appreciate the effort exhibited thus far, and then end the conversation so that the task can be resumed.

Let's take a moment to break down the methodology of this conversation—the first important element is the employee's performance is above expectation. For this reason, it's important to acknowledge, but he or she is aware of the progress, so we don't linger on laudatory feedback. We reassess performance against the objective, and find that early completion is likely, based upon the precedent. This information is supported and shared with the employee, but then we end the conversation. Rather than re-vamping deadlines, we can deduce from performance that this employee is at a comfortable pace and understands the importance of finishing in a timely manner. Out of respect for that performance, we don't micromanage, but do evince an understanding of shorter completion time to encourage the same speed of work and deter potential wasted time. Without obtaining specific measurable progress, even an efficient employee can slow down work speed to avoid an extra task being added. This is one reason creating concrete and definable status checkpoints is essential.

With the same task and deadline, what would happen if at the midpoint, an employee had completed 30 pages? Firstly, we want to acknowledge any work completed to that point. We then need to again break out the math. Stick to the facts—for example, "based upon completing 30 pages in the first 4 hours, we're entering 7.5 pages per hour. We have about four hours left in the day, and with 70 pages remaining, that means we'd need to complete 17.5 pages to complete by the end of day." Probe your employee to understand if there were any circumstances impeding performance. After you present the math, ask if that is a reasonable goal. Chances are, increasing performance by more than 100 percent is not reasonable. It's time to make a judgment call—do you let the agent try to finish, reassign the task completely, bring in another team member to help, take the task on yourself, or move the deadline? Let's assume the deadline is inflexible. Your employee's response may guide the decision. If he or she has a migraine, for example, data entry may not be the best task and reassigning the task may be necessary. If you don't have the workforce, you may need to take on the task yourself. More than likely, the easiest solution is to add in another person. This brings in extra hands but keeps an agent working who already knows the task. As a bonus, you can compare work speeds. Split the remaining pages evenly, 35 to each person, and add in another checkpoint. Expected measurable performance was not met the first time, so it's important to add that checkpoint, perhaps after two hours. Again, many managers may assume that because a second person was added, the task will be completed. You know that trite saying about what happens when you assume. After two hours, each person should have roughly 17.5 pages done. Check with each briefly, ask what page he or she is on. Appreciate the work done and then evaluate the results. Is the original agent still working at the same speed? Is the second agent brought in working faster, slower, or at the same speed? Depending upon how these questions are answered, you may find that your expectations for which employees are safe options for a task may change. If the second employee reports 70 percent completion while the first employee is around 45 percent, it's important to understand what the cause is behind the disparity, but this is part of end evaluation.

Once the task is completed, it can be helpful to have a short debrief with each employee. Again, acknowledge the accomplishment, and also quickly review the results. You may find that the slower worker has a higher rate of accuracy, which could cause you to re-evaluate your timeframe expectations. The opposite may be true—for example, both employees could have great accuracy, but the second agent simply types faster, or does not have to look at the keyboard when typing. It may also be that the other employee had more bathroom breaks or perhaps was sick. The reasons are various, but without these concrete and measurable checkpoints, you would either find an incomplete task at the end of the day or be unaware of any complications. The moral of the story is *track progress in quantitative terms on items that you delegate to subordinates*.

While the example was short term and relatively concrete, the principle still holds true. For longer projects, you still want measurable checkpoints, but they will likely be spaced farther apart and involve reviewing drafts that will lead to the final project. Consider also your team meetings. Truly, this should take place weekly as a forum both to obtain status reports but also for you to leverage the reasoning behind your delegation choices. Part of the communication piece is that transparency, and it can serve as motivation both for the employee you chose to delegate to as well as those employees seeking additional opportunities. During those meetings, do not shy away from seeking that concrete and measurable status information—if your employees are embarrassed by these questions, there's an issue with their time management. This information is not private or sensitive, so create accountability and your employees will have to strive for those standards. Team meetings can also provide a litmus test for your strength at assessing deadlines. Do your employees on the whole consistently fall short of the expected completion date? This requires careful examination. It's important to understand how your employees spend their work hours, whether they have the skills and tools needed to complete the task, or if their workload is excessively restrictive, all of which are facts you can learn from status reports and checkpoints.

To what degree does all of this translate to peer delegation? It honestly depends upon the scenario. Let's consider a large project where you are effectively the leader but delegate the monthly newsletter to your peer. We both know your involvement doesn't end here. It's still important to create those concrete deadlines and expectations, let's say that the template be created in one week, content filled by week two and a draft submitted by Friday in two weeks. What do those checkpoints sound like? For the template creation, it starts simply with asking on the first week deadline if the template is created. If yes, appreciate and then ask to see the document thus far. As the project leader, you have authority over the products for that task, and that means you can ask for the current project materials at any time.

What happens if your peer does not have the template? It's a delicate balance. You could push the deadline to Monday and ask if he or she can send it then. You could decide to wait until the next Friday, when the full first draft is due. You could create the template yourself, offer to have someone else make the template, or reassign the task. It's important to gauge the reasoning behind the lack of completion. Did your peer forget, is it a busy week, is there a lack of motivation, or is this subversion of your authority on the task? Most problems are easily resolved—you can send a calendar reminder and ask for the template on Monday, or advise you will look at the full draft next Friday. It's in the schedule now, no excuses. In terms of being busy or apathetic, honestly ask your peer if it would be better to have someone else complete the task—empathize with the balancing act that is a manager's workload. The latter and more subtle instance of the peer ignoring your needs on the project may be the most frustrating, but consider your priorities. Rather than wage war for the respect of your peer, remove the point of contention and reassign the task, or complete it yourself. Chances are you know shortcuts to create the newsletter template, and can produce the results you want, and call on others to assist with writing content. You can absolutely share the situation with your direct manager, but indicate that you have simply made other arrangements, as the project outcome is the most important detail. Revoking tasks will send the message that you will not grovel for work to be completed when you ask—and let's be honest, who has time to grovel? Don't delegate to employees that are apathetic, and don't delegate to peers who won't follow through, especially on projects you still retain leadership of.

Now that we've treated potential cases for issues with delegating to peers, let's assume that your peer provides the template by the deadline. If you are happy with the outcome, send your thanks and reconfirm the next deadline and what you will be looking for. In the case of having specific content you want in the newsletter, outline the desired message(s); one distinction is that more latitude may be offered to your peer if there is room for discretion in the content. At the management level and as your equal, a peer you delegate to should be able to contribute value without needing excessive detail, but if you have a clear vision be sure that is communicated.

Jumping to the next checkpoint, let's assume that the submitted draft needs a few revisions and edits, but overall is fitting your expectations. Again, reinforce the positive, be factual about the changes you are looking for, and provide another deadline requesting the finished project. Allow a few days between your deadline and the actual timeframe, so that you can do a final proofing and be sure that the product is one you are proud of. Don't fall victim to the illusion that all managers are created equal—while your peer may be a graphic design genius, there may be need for a grammar aficionado to be sure the written content is professional and correct. Followup will be necessary, especially before submitting the final product when you are the responsible party. It is easy to accept praise for a task your group completed, but hard to receive criticism on an assignment you did not personally work on—for that reason, stay involved and use those checkpoints to ensure quality. The time commitment is minimal, but can avoid disastrous effects, as we saw with the data entry not following the needed timeline.

Similarly to the difference between monitoring progress for an employee versus a peer, the process is also slightly different when monitoring delegation for a manager. To a degree, you can absolutely ask for a status update, but keep in mind that a respectful tone and sticking to the facts is still imperative. If you need business data that only your manager has and have delegated retrieving that data, give yourself a timeline based on that conversation. It can be difficult to ask for a concrete deadline from your manager, but consider the alternative. Without knowing your manager's time commitments for the day or week, you may underestimate how busy he or she is, and then when you check in it could appear impatient. Set a timeline, for example explain that you appreciate getting that data and ask if it would be possible to have by end of day. If your boss is amenable, offer to send a calendar invitation; the initiative on your part is noted and who doesn't appreciate having one less thing to remember? Include yourself on the reminder and set the deadline approximately 30 minutes before end of day. This will avoid asking your boss once the computer is shut down for the day. Should the documents not be received by then, you can choose to send an instant message, a follow-up email, or just walk over. Evaluate how your boss usually asks you for information, and consider the task at hand. You may benefit from sending the IM if you know your manager responds quickly, as you can then stay at your desk, communicate in real-time, and confirm receipt of the document via email. Conversely, if your boss is an in-person communicator, consider reciprocating that style and visit the office. Evaluate how busy your boss appears—should you exchange pleasantries, or is there clearly a lot going on that day that would suggest getting to the point? Managers appreciate this kind of assessment on your part, and if it's been a busy day, just the sight of your face might offer reminder of the missing data files. Stick to the facts to maintain the professional tone when your manager owes you work, and don't hesitate to set those concrete timeframes to have clear expectations on both sides.

Regardless of how simple the task, having measurable expectations can help avoid missed deadlines or inferior results. Follow these suggestions to manage your team, your expectations, and the tasks you delegate:

1. Even the small tasks need checkpoints that provide quantitative statuses.

2. If your checkpoint reveals less than satisfactory progress, you can make changes to still be successful.

3. When you are accountable for the project results, even peers and managers need concrete checkpoints.

4. Checkpoints allow for evaluation of performance against expectations and reflection on performance, as well as your perceptions versus reality.

DELEGATION VS. MICROMANAGEMENT

"Never tell people how to do things. Tell them what to do and they will surprise you with their ingenuity."

- Gen. George S. Patton

It's an elemental paradox. You don't want to do all the work personally, but you want it to look to your management as if you did. It's the other end of the continuum from "I do all the work and he gets all the credit." Acknowledging the contributions of a team is another subject, but as managers of any stripe, we are responsible for more work than we can personally perform.

There's a trick to it—and it's not sleight-of-hand. The "trick" is a five-letter word called "trust." For any delegated project to be successfully completed by a subordinate, a word-of-bond must be established along the functioning hierarchy—what the military calls "the chain of command."

Being able to delegate and keep your fingers out of the pie demands open doors, open communication, an understanding of the delegate's motivations, and the assumed responsibility of the delegate to advise the delegator of anticipated difficulties in time for the delegator to bring personal or organizational resources to bear.

The paradox thickens. You want to delegate the task, but you also must delegate the authorities. To expect a subordinate to make decisions on which you can depend, you must provide that subordinate with only general, not specific guidance.

Define the Language

There is a divergence of interest in any delegated process. The delegator is aware that while he may not be involved in the execution of that process, the ultimate responsibility will remain his. The delegator is aware that there is a fragility of communication between him and the lowest level on which any task—or any portion of a task—has been levied.

Like it or not, whether there are problems in the process or the project at hand isn't of interest to top management; the "proof is in the pudding," to use a cliché. Irrespective of the problems that have provided roadblocks along the road from project inception to project conclusion, the facts remain that (1) the project was considered "doable," (2) the people were considered capable, (3) the expectations were considered reasonable, and (4) the product of was considered deliverable. The wise manager at any level must ensure that there is a working product on delivery day, and that all the signs point toward successful completion as the schedule closes in on that day.

The questions that now arise are these: if the project was not considered "doable" with the resources available, were steps taken to acquire additional resources? If the people's skills were insufficient, were there qualified new hires or at least the reallocation of talent that would bring the potential within the realm of capability? Are the expectations fully reasonable or are they someone's "pipe dream?" How often has it happened that because someone in power gets a buzz in the bonnet, an attempt to do the impossible is begun before anybody ever asks the question?

An insurance company in Connecticut experienced this firsthand. Pressed to provide timely online processing of customer applications, the assigned project group had encountered what seemed to be an insurmountable roadblock: somebody at a high level—someone with power but little understanding of the problem—had mandated a 10-second response time. The IT people scrambled, but the very best they could do was 30 seconds, and even that wasn't consistent.

The "expert" happened to be at a location in California, so he came to Hartford to try to overcome the problem. After working on it for three days, he was convinced that the most improvement that could be made would be to average 25 seconds. Frustrated, he climbed back onto the airplane to California.

Enroute, he arrived at a solution that he felt would improve the response time, but it wasn't something that he could just lay out in a memo. He notified the IT people he was coming back to Connecticut. Once back, he encountered the project manager who boasted that *he* could meet the 10-second requirement, while the "expert's" solution could only trim the time to 15 seconds. The duel was now on, and benchmarks proved that the expert could beat even the 15-second mark. Nonplussed, the in-house IT person boasted again that *he* could match the requirement. "But your solution didn't work," said the expert of the IT member's effort. "If mine doesn't *have* to work, I can beat it even further."

What this little story demonstrates is that when an unreasonable expectation is established, there is a distinct possibility that the people charged with meeting that expectation will play along with it until failure is so obvious that, having expended so much time, money, and energy, the "less than perfect solution" ends up becoming implemented.

What's At Risk?

Managers are guilty of taking on projects that will make them look good, rather than those whose contributions to the organization are significant. The phrase *indict the innocent; promote the responsible* is more real than imagined. The situation is somewhat like a major league athlete who is rewarded for outstanding performance. The difference is that when the batting crown is given out, it's given to the batter. There is no support group that takes over the day-to-day functions of swinging the bat on this player's behalf.

Yet if the team does not play well, it is the manager who is dismissed, the rationale being that a worker not well led is not solely responsible for the performance of the team. It therefore follows, in the organizational world, that everything delegated to anyone is a direct reflection upon the manager who makes the delegation. It then invites that person to "bird dog" every possible action such that its on-time and perfect execution would enhance his personal reputation. Sadly, the world doesn't operate that way.

Here's How to Get into Trouble

Micromanagement is the easiest thing in the world to do, and is highly dependent on the manager's ego. All you need to do is to insert yourself into every facet of the work being done. Of course, the rest of your work may not be completed, but if you see this particular project or process as your step into an elevated future, there are many things to do. We know this: there are many ways to do it wrong. Consider:

- Depend on yourself alone. Your management came to you because you "know about this stuff," or with some form of confidence in you, hopefully earned. To get you excited about taking on the project, you are "slapped on the back," literally or figuratively, and heralded to the rest of the organization as the "whiz kid" who will get the organization out of its dilemma. Yes, we know that you have subordinates and that some of your subordinates will assist you, but really, you're the person who will see this done. This now tempts you to think that you are the only one on which you can depend. You just increased your workload.

- It follows that if you are solely responsible, you will be able to solve all the problems yourself. You must make certain that no major decisions are made without your input. You not only know *a* solution, you are convinced you know *the* solution that best fits the problem.

- Don't allow subordinates to take on interesting tasks where they know you can use their help. After all, if they do that, they might demonstrate that they can be trusted to do the work.

- Instruct any workers in the processes to follow your lead and do it in the greatest detail possible. You want not only to dictate the conclusion, you want to ensure that *they* will do the job in precisely the same manner as *you* would do the job, because that's the way it is *supposed* to be done. You are, after all, the expert—that's how you got here in the first place. One variation of this is that you must insist on uniform contributions, feeling that "x" hours must, by definition, produce "y" units of output, and therefore "z" completed units.

- Intimidate all subordinates with your exceptional knowledge and experience. Create the impression that no matter what they do, it won't be good enough to satisfy you or your superiors.

- Insist on being consulted at every fork in the road. Direction is your responsibility also. Yes, the product is important, but it must be seen that you are providing superlative supervision, so having a hand in direction is paramount.

- Assume that your delegate's exceptional confidence is reflected in your attitudes. Your subordinates, after all, exist to make you look good in the eyes of your superiors.

- Insist on being notified before decisions are made. Total control is the idea, so there is no decision too small to merit your consideration. Better yet, be at the decision point when a direction has been selected or consensus has been reached, such that you have your imprimatur placed upon it. Nobody should be allowed to make individual decisions.

- If you have detailed the processes, you must review others' contributions thoroughly. One way to do this is to set a deadline in advance of the one that has been established for you to allow you time to "fix" all the problems you are certain you will find.

- Create an "us" vs. "them" project orientation. This is especially true when the process you are creating will be used in another part of the organization. You know that the ultimate user of your process wants the data to be presented in a certain way, but you think you know better. What you're building is a thing of beauty, and as John Keats once opined, "A thing of beauty is a joy forever." From 1972 to 1999, there existed in this country a computer manufacturer known as Control Data. With software written by Seymour Cray, who went on to develop supercomputers, the company refused to make minor changes to its operating systems to satisfy user's needs. Company customers were accused of wanting to finger-paint on the Mona Lisa. Did you catch that the company no longer exists?

- Become "Meeting Happy." Meet with your subordinates en masse at least once each week and with the critical members at least once each day. Control all meetings. Ensure that the meeting minutes are recorded such that you can keep your finger on the pulse of progress and "sanitize" any observations that might flow upward in the organization, particularly those that might reflect poorly on you.

- Keep downward communication at a minimum, with one exception: pass on all communication that increases the performance pressures on the work group, and if that communication is insufficient, add some of your own.

- Keep upward communication only that which is necessary to plead for resources and justify the lack of progress. However, broadcast all your successes. This will guarantee your maximum beneficial exposure to your superiors.

- Control the methods of communication. One way to do this is to require contributors to make a progress report—but, before any progress report is sent upward, make sure you edit them so that only the "good news" is sent upward. Management doesn't want to know what the problems are. The final reports before the planned project delivery would seem to be sufficient.

- Direct all course corrections. You absolutely need to be informed and approve any changes. You wouldn't want to have to rely on someone else to "make it right."

- Hand out only administrative tasks and oversee their production. People love paperwork, especially when there has been little progress in the project. It fosters an atmosphere of creative writing. Since it provides little opportunity for personal growth or skills improvement, it will allow you to focus on your direct involvement.

- Work the oversight of your subordinates' projects into your schedule. One advantage of this process is that it allows you to work significant overtime or perhaps even take some considerable work to your home. This will allow you to jump in and take over when you sense any difficulty, and it creates an atmosphere where mistakes are punishable offenses. In fact, go to great lengths to demonstrate that you don't make mistakes, and therefore they should not make mistakes as well.

- Pick up the slack from underperforming employees. This will allow you to place the same unrealistic expectations on your subordinates as you place on yourself.

- Resist delegation. You don't look good when others are doing work that you think represents your personal future. For that reason, also don't let anybody work "on their own." If you can't be with the person doing the work, detail another employee to keep you apprised.

- Set unreasonable deadlines. If you do that, you may be assured that things are done on time. Check the progress of the project regularly by visiting or making queries. Better yet, require daily update e-mails that you can print and file in the project folder. If it happens that the project collapses, you will now be able to present evidence that nobody ever told you it was in trouble.

- You must assume all workers are capable, irrespective of what you have observed. If you involve yourself in the details and make all necessary corrections, it will work, you feel. Make sure that you retrieve delegated work if you don't think it's going well.

- Prevent others from assuming responsibility. Making and taking responsibility for decisions cause people to grow. If you will hoard all opportunities to excel and take them for yourself, you will be able to disempower your subordinates. This will allow crisis mode to flourish and you (and Mighty Mouse) can swoop in to "save the day."

- Institute instant feedback to ensure that your team has made progress. Do it regularly and there will be no time to work on the project, but that might be counterproductive.

- Sweat the details – who needs time to analyze, plan, communicate, monitor, control anyway? Insist on reports of activity before you deal with your people directly. This will cause you to appear to be very serious about change and improvement. If you don't help them to grow, you can ensure that you'll never be replaced, at least until you develop that heart attack.

- Don't credit subordinate insights. You can do this by not listening.

If you do all this religiously, be prepared one day to see something like this affixed to an office wall:

The Flogging Will Continue Until Morale Improves

Are these enough "horror stories" thus far to cause you to question the benefits of micromanagement?

Let's look now to the advisory side of the question.

If you're a smart manager, you only way upward is to ensure that should you be tapped for a promotion, someone on the team that you have must be prepared to take over. After all, getting a promotion is a new opportunity for you—why should your approach not be finding ways to develop your team and therefore your replacement?

You don't want a promotion? Nothing wrong with that. Finding your niche and being successful at it is something to be desired. However, think of this: today's motorist has little concept of chokes, throttles, or governor. Throttles were designed to control the passage of flow of fuel to an engine. Chokes were designed to control the amount of air inserted into a carburetor, no longer necessary with fuel-injection engines. However, a governor was something different. Everything had to pass through the governors. A governor restricted the fuel flow and therefore the speed of the vehicle. Not so many years ago, auto manufacturers installed them and wouldn't remove them for a few thousand miles. Not so many years ago, the wild teen-aged driver was held in check until he had gained sufficient experience to remove the device. If you wish to micromanage, you are attempting to increase the throttle (speed) while placing a choke on the ability of your group and a governor on just how successful your group may become.

Nobody faults the unsure manager for wanting things to go right— and perhaps even better than right, for no reason other than his or her reputation. If you're reluctant to delegate, you have abandoned your ability to focus on the entire project and to concentrate on the larger picture. Keep your direct involvement in the project to a minimum and you can focus on the exceptions, running interference for the team that is marching toward project completion.

Let's be honest. Micromanaging is fun. It's safe. It's comfortable. It "keeps our hands in." The problem is that it requires your 100% attention. If you would like your managerial life to be so highly focused on minutiae, then keep at it. If, on the other hand, you wish for your people to grow and for you to take advantage of new opportunities for your own growth, it would behoove you to examine how you operate.

Here's The Plan

It's time for a little introspection.

Micromanagement will produce a low-performance team—for many reasons. Delegation permits the utmost in performance.

You have been declared a manager. It's time you recognized two things: (1) nobody needs a manager if there are no problems to manage, and (2) your success in your organization is highly dependent on your ability to perform more work than is humanly possible, and therefore that work must be achieved through the efforts of others. That has something to say for goal setting, performance measurement, and achievement rewards.

Some questions:

- How is your turnover? People unhappy with you will seek to replace you, generally by seeking another position, often within the same facility, but more often with another. Bear in mind also that high turnover is apparent on its surface—your boss, the human relations department, and everybody from your position upward knows it's happening. If it happens too much, where will they look? After all, if the baseball season has been bad, the manager is sacked.

- Are there evidences of black humor appearing? One is presented above, but that merely touches the surface. A low morale level brings on a sense of futility, and people who otherwise could make meaningful contributions begin to look for a place to go. If they are not successful, at least initially, the work will experience a "slowdown," as your team's lethargy builds. Lethargy begets apathy, and eventually the secret is out.

- Are your people providing work of lower quality than you know they can produce? Disheartened team members will often "go along to get along." It's easier, requires no challenges, lowers expectations, and keeps their positions safe while they look for other challenges. If they're smart, they may be going through the paces merely the keep the paycheck and security. The danger in this approach is that the highly motivated workers find another station while you're left with the low-performing team members. What happens now? You now must get involved in the work. The rest of your duties fall by the wayside. Your own performance ratings sink.

- Have you lost your ability to affect profitability? What about the productivity of your group—assuming that you measure it? What about your responsibility for new business? If you are so heavily involved in working *in* the business that you have no time to work *in behalf* of the business, would it surprise you to see that your business will stay level, at least, and decline is a distinct possibility. If you're an upper-level manager reading this, what will be the impact of several project groups that have become moribund?

- Have you considered how you have established priorities? The individual elements of a task list are not of equal priority, or are they necessarily sequential. If everything is of equal priority, the organization is faced with running off in all directions at once. That might be good for a grinding wheel, but of no value at all for a project-oriented staff in an up-and-coming business.

- What about you? Is it affecting your family life? Is it affecting the family lives of your subordinates? If you are forcing subordinates to make those choices, you may have results in the short term, but in the end, family will win out. The result is delayed, damaged, or incomplete projects. The further result is your career has come to a standstill. You can't be promoted because you are indispensable where you are.

Are You Ready To Change?

We began this treatise with the word *trust*. That's where the micromanaging-to-delegation shift must begin. You must find a way to impart trust to your subordinates; you must convince them, by your actions, to trust you. Here are some ways this can be done:

- Planning is important. Ask the workgroup to plan the tasks. Ask them to establish objectives (goals, methods, and measurements). Delegate an observer within the group whose responsibility will be to acquaint the members of variations in time to ensure that what is reported upward matches the initial, or even the revised plan, that has been developed for the project.

- Don't just hand out the routine assignments, the stuff you cannot or do not want to do. Offer the staff some of the plum jobs. You know they are there. One way to do this is to put them on a bid system. Don't merely ask them how long they think they might take to do something, ask them to plan it out, schedule it, and document it as a proposal. How you choose to evaluate that proposal may vary, of course, but it causes some of those creative minds to work. You may well discover that different people perceive the problem uniquely. This process will not only tell you whose interest is high but also who considers themselves competent. If you draw low interest, you will need next to evaluate skills, for it may be that you will have to undergo some training before the task can begin.

- If it is true that an employee's reach must be beyond his or her grasp, then it behooves you, as manager, to make assignments that are just beyond the known capability of the subordinate. In this manner, the employee will know enough to tackle the assignment while recognizing that new knowledge is required. You, then, as manager, will then have to help the employee obtain the knowledge. People being trained to take on more challenging assignments tend to have higher morale. Be aware, however, that even if you help them gain the skills, it will be of no consequence if they are not allowed, permitted, or required to use them. Further, new skills bequeath increased value; ensure that growth possibilities exist in salary considerations.

- Let out the leash gradually. Assign the responsibility and then watch, and when it becomes apparent that something more is needed, assign the decision-making requirements. Don't merely allow your employees to make low-level or minor decisions; go for broke. Give them permitted steps that they can take on their own. If a budget is needed to provide fiscal spending authority, give that out, as well.

- Then watch. Require reporting points to be built into the plan and for these people to make their reports at that time. If they are to make decisions, and particularly if they are to expend resources to get those results, you have the right to know what return comes from those resources, following quickly after their use.

- Spend time with the group developing internal procedures, even if done in an elementary way. Ensure that someone specific is charged with monitoring the work of the project against those procedures. If you fail to meet the checkpoints, meet again and re-plan. If you meet objectives, then laud those who have worked so hard. If you meet them very far in advance, check first to ensure that no shortcuts were taken just to make the project team look good, and then praise them to the rooftops.

Very little done wrong can't be done over, given time and resources. There are very few tasks where a mistake can't be corrected. There are exceptions: handling dynamite and operating a punch press come to mind. Nevertheless, for the most part, things will sometimes go wrong. A knowledgeable monitoring process allows minor course corrections in relative real-time, at least before anything significant has been expended.

Mistakes are always fruitful grounds for discussing what went wrong, why it went wrong, and what you're going to do about it. It is always a training exercise. Don't, however, dash in and "make it all better." If the process gets out of hand, a quick reaction is helpful. Remember the project still has to be completed by the deadline; however, this is not a reason to throw delegation out the window. Pinpoint the problem, let the people decide what should be done about it, and allow them to try their solution. Even if it isn't what you think should be done, it might work.

Keep the door open and the welcome mat out. You're after compatible working relations. Allow extensive and vigorous debate that will bring the force of your subordinates' minds to bear on the project and any problems you may anticipate or encounter. Of course, where possible, work out solutions that everybody can accept.

In an era of iPads, it is now possible to establish reporting platforms that keep everybody informed. It's called the project's *dashboard*. Trust, like a dashboard, is only valuable if it is maintained. If you can convince people to trust you and be willing to give you all the news—good, bad, and ugly—you'll make comfortable progress. Withhold a piece of information and then have somebody discover that you have done so, and you've opened yourself to problems.

That's all good—but....

Until now, we have focused on existing organizations comprised of many people with various skills. Startups have very little of that kind of luxury.

In any new venture, managing and micromanagement are essentially the same tasks. You began your company with a set of skills, and chances are those skills are far from administrative in nature. You know little about how to hire. You know less about how to supervise. You are intrinsically involved in most matters, and except for answering the telephone or typing a business letter, you focus upon what can make the business grow.

There is nothing esoteric in this. You have invested your money, perhaps even your severance pay when you left the last company, because life seemed to be intolerable. Every decision that is made affects your wallet *today*, to say nothing about any future period. So it is natural for you to control all the reins of your business—until, like the others—you find you are simply incapable of doing everything yourself and recognize that if you continue to do so, the company cannot possibly grow beyond a specific point. There is an explosion coming and the sight will not be pretty.

But what do you do? Your widget is in design. The factory is "under construction," often in your own garage, and the big question now is whether to fund the prototype or eat dinner, as you might not be able to afford to do both.

Intergroup Accountability

Is there ever a time when micromanagement is beneficial? Yes, of course. The classic case of micromanagement must be in the military, where supervision, generally a function of acquired rank, is found at every level.

A new startup company would be a good place for

micromanagement, largely because the whole idea of a new operation is a gleam in the proprietor's eye. It's a little more complicated if a partnership team divides major organizational functions; but for at least the early months, it may be necessary. After all, the new product may never have before existed, or if it did, there is something new and different about this iteration. Any firm that gathers as a startup will likely be staffed by technicians who are most intimately associated with the product or process that aligns with the function. It's only after some short period that the new organization begins to realize that what brought these people together was not the desire to administer.

Micromanaging will be most useful where the technical skill must be developed. Research and development firms will take some basic skills and then will build those skills in support of the mission. Sometimes they fail. Sometimes they succeed. Whether the organization succeeds or fails will depend on the learning curve-to-resource allocation mix. Simply stated, macromanagement is possible only if there is an abundance of resources relative to the time demands for the output. If the new venture is "under the gun" for a quick delivery—perhaps for a market deadline, there may not be time to allow the work to happen without the manager getting her fingers dirty.

One other area where micromanagement has an edge: where there is a unique skill or a proprietary process—something where you would not expect many people would already hold qualifications.

Another important point: a manager with a penchant for detail is ill assigned. This would lead to some discussion about just how far a technician can advance without having to move to a managerial position.

The obverse is, of course, macromanagement—looking at and controlling from the "big picture." This may work best in a larger or more established organization. Many such organizations promote from within the company but outside the workgroup. Therefore, the familial liaisons built among project members are not compromised merely because someone has been promoted. This leads to inter-member accountability. The macromanager recognizes this and establishes that accountability. In this manner, one is working on a task while another is verifying the work and therefore the progress.

It's important also to recognize that macromanagement is not aloofness. It assumes the existence of a qualified staff and a program to continue or improve that qualification. The method must be adopted where there are great dissimilarities in the work performed by subordinates.

Now we've come full circle. A manager can macromanage those with whom a bond of trust has been established. Make the team members responsible for using their independence and unique skills; depend on them for their knowledge, competence, and for the validity of the decision-making processes.

It is scary. A manager with a macromanagement style can work himself out of a job simply by proving to his supervision that the world doesn't revolve around him. There's the dichotomy. Do a good job of micromanaging and prove that there is no point to ever promoting you. Do a good job of delegation via macromanaging, and prove that you have trained your replacement.

Is the paradox unworkable? No, not if those who have moved upward recognize that this is the appropriate evolution of the process.

Dr. Lawrence Peter, in his book *The Peter Principle*, stated that a person advances to his level of incompetence. If that is true, any manager is in danger of eclipsing any optimum position in the hierarchy. The idea is to recognize the appropriate career path for *all* individuals and to tailor both the project and the progression around it.

It's Called Bootstrapping

We wouldn't even be discussing micromanagement versus delegation if the problems that confronted us weren't too large for us to handle by ourselves. Be thankful. That's called growth. So now you have employees ... one, two, three. In the short term, you are both "top management" and "project management."

The concept of bootstrapping is that you lay down enough instruction to begin the process. The process, then, is designed to open the vista, the communication, if you will, to the next step. Then the next step is the full operation of the process. The method is analogous to using a starter motor to turn the flywheel, to cause the pistons to operate, and subsequently the fuel gases to compress, where they are shocked and the engine swings into operation.

However, here's an important point. Most who have gone into business for themselves have done so for one of several reasons. Some don't like the regimentation of a structured organization. Some don't like the mundane day-to-day tasks that never seem to disappear. Some simply want to do things where they can have fun and still earn a living. Many have done so because they simply wish to control their own destinies.

Hiring people correctly in the first place will facilitate any organizational process, and a whole body of knowledge exists on the best and most productive ways to match an employee to the tasks that must be completed while making an effort to satisfy both the organizational and individuals' desires.

It therefore follows that if you have taken the correct steps to obtain and place the proper people in the appropriate tasks, their growth as employees and your progress as a manager will come from your knowledge of just when you should become involved and to what extent. Nobody is suggesting that you delegate and then disappear. That won't work either, and is certain to produce disappointing results on delivery day.

What we do know is that if you give a ship to the sailor and teach him how to run with the wind, the sailor becomes an acceptable captain. He's had the opportunity to try to do it the way he thinks best and if he's not satisfied in the result, to try yet another way. That's the environment of freedom that you must foster. If you can assign the task, keep your fingers out of it, and watch the employee demonstrate his knowledge and motivation, you will be pleasantly surprised at the results. So will *your* boss.

Learn a new word, if it is not in your vocabulary: dichotomy. In definition, this is a difference in opinion, often when the opinions are opposed. The way the employee may do the job may not be the way you do the job, but isn't the real issue that the job is completed and that the function of the process works as was intended?

Give your people time and give them space. Establish report and checkpoints. Don't ignore them—that is not good management, either. However, do allow them freedom to experiment and to gain results from their own perspectives. Then watch them. William Ouchi, in his book *Theory Z*, calls this "management by walking around." Observe them. Make innocent inquiries. Show your interest in their processes of managing their tasks. They don't need you to control what is going on. They merely need to know that you are watching. Then, when the project is done, shout it from the rooftops, and even if you can't grant them a great end-of-year bonus, give them the emotional "bennies" that will ensure this kind of project support will continue.

There is one more consideration. Nobody wants to work with another person, particularly one with fiscal control, looking over his or her shoulder. Consider the plight of the individual forced to work for the micromanager. At what point does frustration show? What about anger? What about negative reactions? Then, at what point does the project that is being micromanaged simply bog down under its own weight? Unhappy project members have been known to sabotage their own efforts under extreme pressure. Ask any upper-level manager who has watched lengthy project estimates made simply because that manager has a history of unreasonably attempting to force the work to be done faster. In this manner, a task is estimated for a month, even though the team may know that it can be done in two weeks. The pressure is gone and if it comes in within those two weeks, the team looks heroic. If it does not, there is defensible "wiggle room."

How many worthwhile projects are sacrificed on the altar of expediency? How many people will go home tonight, turn on their computers, and call up their resumés?

Assign the work. Monitor the progress. Troubleshoot the areas that only you can solve. Leave the team alone to find ways to do the work. Then praise them all for a job well done.

RECOGNIZING THOSE YOU DELEGATE TO

"No man will make a great leader who wants to do it all himself, or to get all the credit for doing it."

- Andrew Carnegie

After the delegated task is complete, a simple "thank you" should do the trick, right? Not necessarily. Like many of the other principles we've discussed, recognition is grossly underutilized and undervalued. Don't make that same mistake. Recognition serves many functions, including expressing your gratitude, showing the delegate appreciation for the work he or she has done, and in some cases making sure others know where credit is due. Managers who recognize their delegates strengthen those interpersonal relationships, which can provide more opportunities for both parties. It is much easier to ask for help after already working with an individual and building rapport through recognition. Most businesses are meritocracies, so based upon that concept, rewards and recognition based upon performance are perfectly in line with the business model. As children we are taught to grasp for the best grade, the affirmation of our work, and this continues into adulthood. Handing out gold stars may be a hallmark of the past, but recognition is very much alive in the present, and the visibility both for a person doing great work and a leader taking time to recognize accomplishments benefits both parties.

There are multitudes of ways to recognize your delegate, so the first concept to internalize is *make the recognition proportionate to the task.* If your employee agonized over a long term assignment that required enormous effort and innovation, "thank you" will probably seem a bit cheap. While verbal appreciation should always be present, tasks far above and beyond the norm require appreciation beyond the norm. Conversely, if your employee just finished distributing that memo to everyone's desks, throwing a parade might be overkill. Keep in mind, too, that recognition is an opportunity to communicate the logic behind the praise—to avoid favoritism, keeping the reward in proportion with the task shows strong analytical skills. Don't be afraid to recognize your delegate in front of the team, but provide background on what the hubbub is about, and what that specific individual brought to the project. The same principle applies to management meetings—taking the time to offer verbal recognition in front of the team increases visibility and is flattering for the delegate, be it your peer or manager. Moreover, (and this is a fringe benefit, not a driving factor), consider how taking this initiative reflects on you: strength in public speaking, humility, team mentality, leadership and delegation skills are all evinced when you take a few moments to acknowledge those who help "make it happen." Truly, delegation is a symbiotic process, when done correctly, and even recognition succumbs to that rule.

In addition to the verbal recognition we have discussed, how else can we recognize our delegates? Often something in writing is used, and with good reason. This provides concrete documentation of the person's work, your appreciation of that effort, and allows for the accolade to be shared with others in event of applying for promotions or building a portfolio. A less-utilized written acknowledgment is a hand-written note. The time and physical effort makes these notes likely to be saved as motivation. The novelty of a hand-written note also sticks with the recipient, be it your employee, peer or manager. Alternately, written recognition can be as simple as a group email cc'ing the right people, which can have a waterfall effect, drawing out other praise for the delegate's work. For example, recognizing your peer in management while cc'ing the rest of the team and senior management provides a concrete reminder that extraordinary work took place, and hitting "reply all" to add to that praise is about as easy as recognition gets. Emails can offer instant gratification, can be printed or saved, and can reach parties who are out of the office or located at another site. To reach far, you need only reach for the keyboard.

Keep in mind when writing any sort of laudatory message or missive, the language and phrasing is a reflection of you. This means a grammatically correct, properly formatted document in professional font. Additionally, the text should not simply read "Thanks to Julie for her work on the department newsletter." Get specific! It's important to outline how this person drove results, what unique strengths he or she brought to the task, and this will clarify the reason behind the recognition. For instance: "Julie single-handedly created a dynamic template for the newsletter, organized unique and engaging content, and managed the completion and editing of the newsletter on a monthly basis to ensure employees at all levels are aware of business news." You can then add the appreciative comments, but giving the specific examples is key to meaningful recognition. This is true not only for your employees, but also in instances of delegating to your peer or manager. Everyone enjoys receiving kudos for a job well done, especially when senior management is included on the message.

While emails provide a quick means of distributing recognition, there are times when a more formal mode is appropriate. Consider the employee who has piloted a process change affecting notable client satisfaction improvements and cost savings. An email simply won't do. Your company may have a formal award process in place for these instances, so you can absolutely defer to that process. Many systems have an automatic reward that is sent to both the recipient and his or her manager, which is a nice way to spread the news about great work. If possible, still print out a copy of these certificates, or if someone else awards your agent, print those notices. The effort to make a physical copy as well as the tangible item add effort to an otherwise simplified process, and effort is often as important as the act when it comes to recognition. You may also be able to nominate your employee for a larger company award that involves a ceremony or formal dinner—if the task or project warrants the work to create the nomination, it's well worth the while. Visibility is another huge factor in these rewards, so if your business has a formal process, be sure to take advantage.

In case your business world does not have a recognition system— it's time for you to do some leg work. A formal certificate or plaque certainly wouldn't be out of the question, or perhaps a business lunch with management to recognize the agent formally. You may even be able to swing a monetary award. Without a preexisting structure for recognition, evaluate the task completed and resultant benefits, then approach your manager about the need for more significant compensation or reward. Tasks that qualify for such recognition should be less common, so taking steps to appropriately reward should be possible. In environments lacking a rewards structure, you can even suggest levels of recognition and a formalized process to regulate and ensure kudos are given. From the simple certificate to an awards ceremony or dinner, there is a spectrum of recognition, so keep that proportion concept in mind. Your company may even have a rewards points system, which can be redeemed for company logo merchandise or gift cards—giving those points equates to a tangible item, which is also a great token of recognition. On the smaller side of recognition, perhaps for a data entry task that was simple enough but just a long process, consider tokens with a motivational saying or message. These tasks likely offered a break from the usual job tasks, so receiving a token in recognition is more than sufficient. You can even attach a relevant candy to make a pun, and sugar is always a good boost for morale!

To help encourage group performance, you can even institute a trophy of sorts (perhaps a telephone spray-painted gold for a call center, a bedazzled calculator for the accounting department, etc.) Having bragging rights and a trophy for the week or month for being top performer not only rewards but motivates. While it may seem trivial, the message behind winning is the integral piece—communicate the logic behind why a specific person won, what the trophy means, and what you look for when determining the recipient. This will give your team goals to aim for. In a more varied environment, where agents have such distinct roles it complicates choosing a single winner, opt for a "Hall of Fame" and choose specific tasks or projects that land a person on that wall. You can have multiple recipients, include a favorite quote for each recipient, or even a suggestion for how to exceed in that role, straight from the star performer. The individual recognition and value for ideas is almost as rewarding as having your picture displayed for all to see.

Outside of more tangible methods of recognition, let's think outside the box. Consider not only the finished product, but how the delegate worked on the task. Was he or she entirely self-governed? Did you find that questions came with suggested solutions, rather than a cry for help? Finding a skilled and autonomous employee who can produce results sometimes warrants more attention on your part. Have a serious conversation, starting with acknowledging those behaviors you observed, and ask about the agent's career goals. Create a road map and offer suggestions of building blocks that can further the employee's progress. This may mean finding projects owned by other managers so that agent can gain exposure, or volunteering for a task that interfaces with other departments or locations. Who wants more work as a reward? Your driven employee. While having a reliable, creative, intelligent and self-motivated star on your team is convenient, don't let your needs overwhelm the agent's career opportunities. If you have an honest conversation about development, the employee will recognize the added work for what it is—an opportunity, and a vote of confidence. This type of recognition will not apply to each of your team members, but for appropriate cases it will be more appreciated than a certificate or money. Evaluate what motivates each person on your team—tangible items, praise from management, or the chance to learn new things and grow. This will also help guide your mode of recognition. Your company may have a development program that trains agents in management or other special skills to help advance within the company. If not, this may be another opportunity to create, giving the employee a learning experience and also making a notable leadership move on your part.

Creating a culture of recognition helps to retain employees and boosts morale; the sad truth is that many employees leave companies when they are not compensated for their effort or if they are not being challenged in the role. Delegation and recognition can help alleviate both concerns, as it offers challenging new tasks and appreciation for a job well done. Once you understand the benefits of delegation and recognition, they will become larger parts of your role, whether it's simply sending a thank you note to a colleague for fixing a technical issue, or having the senior manager stop over to congratulate your team on a job well done. Here's a breakdown of some successful recognition methods:

1. A handwritten note

2. An email cc'ing upper management

3. Certificate or Plaque

4. Formal Ceremony/ Dinner

5. Lunch with Management

6. Team Trophy

7. Hall of Fame

8. Quotes with candy

9. New Projects

10. Leadership Opportunities

UNSUCCESSFUL DELEGATION

"I have not failed. I've just found 10,000 ways that won't work."

- Thomas A. Edison

Maybe you've taken careful steps to select the best task for delegation, chosen the right person, provided a concrete deadline, and used in-depth questions to track progress. Or, perhaps you delegated a task haphazardly, under the pressure of time constraints and an unmanageable workload. For a variety of reasons, unsuccessful delegation happens. You are not the only person who has experienced it, but you can take a unique approach to the situation. Remember that as a manager, everyone makes mistakes, but what distinguishes a leader is the action following the error.

The first consideration is to evaluate the status of the task or project. Unsuccessful delegation could mean that the final product is unsatisfactory, that the task is unfinished by the deadline, or that the delegate has done no work. Your first instinct should be to prioritize the situation. If the project is unfinished, it needs to be completed. This may mean an unexpected late night on your part, either finishing the task on your own or pulling together a team and monitoring the progress. In either instance, get the work done. The same principle holds for a task turned in that you are not satisfied with. Your employee should show you the final draft, which you have ultimate say over, so if you are looking at a poorly organized newsletter with excessive grammatical errors you already commented on, unsuccessful delegation has happened. The employee you delegated to either does not have the skill set or did not take care to resolve those issues, although you gave directions for corrections to make. Step in and either fix those items yourself or specifically designate a person to review and make changes. You can then work with the alternate employee to explain exactly what you need completed, but the main point is that *completing the task takes priority*.

Whether for issues of quality or incompleteness, there will be a need to provide feedback to the original delegate, but ensure that this does not impede the project. Consider also your role in the unsuccessful delegation. If you chose a task that was difficult to begin with, be sure to speak with your employee about that factor to rebuild trust. No one likes to feel that they are set up to fail; be sure to mention that you know this was a difficult task, and it was part of the learning process. In order to grow we often face challenges, and some outcomes are more successful than others.

Unsuccessful delegation is not unique to subordinates—it can also happen with your peers and even your manager. More than likely you will hear that the work is not completed because of being too busy or forgetting the task. We have already treated ways to avoid the "I forget," but assuming this was prior to learning concrete deadlines and checkpoints, the final deadline can appear with no corresponding work. It may be uncomfortable, but remember that you are responsible for this work, if you are leading a project and delegated that task. Empathize and express that you definitely understand the business and constraints of the job, but this task has to be completed. Ask questions about whether the manager can pull in an extra agent to complete the task that same day. If the task is too large to complete in that timeframe, or the manager refuses, it's time to refocus energy first on finding a way to finish the job. It may be after the deadline, so consult with the person in charge to explain the situation. This will be the time when you accept full responsibility for the work not being done. As a leader, you made the decision to delegate, and therefore the accountability is yours, regardless of who failed to complete the task. You may need to regain trust from that individual, which is often the greatest negative outcome of unsuccessful delegation, but having a transparent discussion about your choice to delegate can be helpful. Explain the logic behind the circumstances. If you did not use checkpoints or deadlines, include a reflective portion to show that not only are you culpable, but you have already determined ways to avoid these issues in future. Part of leadership is failing, but your grace and attitude in facing failure to complete a task or achieve an objective defines you as a leader.

Perhaps the most uncomfortable unsuccessful delegation is when your manager does not complete a task. Let's assume that in your work environment, you were away on vacation, so your manager was responsible for signing timecards for employee pay. If this did not happen, focus on resolving the issue at hand. This may involve calling your payroll center, signing the timecards yourself, and having a meeting about the event. Focus first on the solution, providing timeframes based upon what your payroll administrator has explained, for example, clarifying that a standard week's pay will be deposited, with any corrections following on the subsequent pay cycle. After explaining the salient facts that impact your employees, apologize. This is where many managers will attempt to gain some empathy by displacing blame, but a leader will simply indicate that although the task was delegated in your absence, it was clearly not completed, and you deeply apologize for the impact to each of your team members. At this point, work to regain trust. Explain that in future, there will be additional measures to ensure this does not happen again. Unless there are any questions, that should be the end of the discussion. You may need to take the time to call employees not in the office, as this can impact financial matters, and making that effort will also work to regain trust. Be certain with failed delegation that you prioritize results and indicate the situation has created more awareness of steps to avoid similar occurrences in future, but as a leader, you should absolutely not blame others when discussing the unsuccessful delegation to the impacted party.

Now that you've taken responsibility for the failed delegation, noted learning opportunities, and avoided playing the blame game, it's time to examine the follow up process with your delegate. It's not as bad as it seems. Before you go into the conversation, take stock of the assignment and conversations you had. Be honest with yourself—was this task appropriate for the delegate? Did you set clear expectations, checkpoints, provide a deadline and enough instructions for the delegate to be successful? Did the delegate seem engaged in being included in the task? If you answer "no" to any of these questions, consider your part in the unsuccessful delegation. Reflection is a hallmark of great leaders—not only do they commit themselves to an objective, but there is a review of the steps leading to outcomes, evaluation of alternatives, and consideration of the result after the fact. If hindsight is 20-20, we need to review the past with clarity so that we move forward stronger and more knowledgeable. In this case, that means evaluating how we contributed to the failure of a project that was delegated. Once you have an understanding of your part in the lack of success, it's time to gain the delegate's perspective.

With a subordinate, these conversations can be intimidating for the individual. Unless you are taking disciplinary action, make a concerted effort to alleviate any fears at the outset of the conversation. Nervousness can diminish the ability to focus on information presented, so clear the air. Now, start by asking questions. It's important to see if your delegate can identify causes leading to the unsuccessful completion of a task and this is essential to your employee's growth. Ask the employee to evaluate how successful the task was, what he or she would have done differently, what you could have done differently, and how satisfied he or she was with the finished product. This step engages the analytical side of the employee's faculties, also pushing nerves to the periphery as we focus on the facts. Several possibilities arise with this step: you may find that your employee simply does not care to talk about the project and demonstrates little concern for the outcome; alternatively, you may find that the employee identifies an awareness of the shortcomings of the finished work, or the employee may not communicate any realization of the failure. In the first case, you need to evaluate the benefit of continuing to probe for information; this employee clearly is detached, and you may need to examine more of the feelings toward extra projects or the employee's mindset, then provide short feedback about the task. If the employee is aware of deficiencies, probe further. On points where you agree, acknowledge your consensus with that assessment, and then examine the question of what could have been done differently.

Most employees will examine their own behaviors, but this is a key moment to demonstrate the principle of "managing up." If the employee does not specifically detail what you could have done differently, ask them directly what you could have done, then why he or she did not take this step. This can open some very honest conversation about the nature of the manager and employee relationship. While you are responsible for overseeing and delegating, the employee is also a key player in that he or she must communicate needs or concerns, even as it relates to your decisions. There are, of course, etiquette guidelines for these interactions, but expressing concerns or needs can mean the difference between a great project and a total failure. This may also be a valuable question to ask your apathetic employee. Start by inquiring if there were any concerns about the task, and follow up with asking why these weren't voiced. You may learn some difficult truths about the perception of you as a manager, but without this feedback, no change could take place. This is a growth opportunity for both yourself and the employee, so be sure to maintain composure, allow grievances to be aired, and take note of the feedback. It may be that you entire team is not aware of the "managing up" idea, which can create a dynamic change in your environment. By giving legitimacy to employee opinion, you allow for a dialectic exchange that can impassion your team, engender improved processes, and provide you with a better knowledge of your team (leading to successful delegation choices in the future).

The final piece of this feedback is the clueless employee. You can attempt to draw out insight and catalyze reflection, but whether through playing dumb or truly not recognizing the implications of the task's failure, you may need to take a didactic approach. As always, *stick to the facts*. You can refer back to the project for specific flaws and ask concrete questions that require an answer. Provide multiple suggestions for what could have been done differently, and ask the employee to choose one and explain why that would be a good option. Still have that conversation about managing up—your employee may or may not grasp the concept, but at its most basic concept, anyone can understand having dialogue about concerns with management.

These conversations can be similar with your peers, but should require less leading. Rather than starting with the probing questions, set up a meeting in private and begin by outlining your role in the failure of the project, as well as the reason for the failure. Explain that you are looking to gain some perspective on how to avoid this in future and ask your peer—what do you think contributed to the outcome? If this is related to time management, you may hear about a heavy workload or forgetting, so follow up with suggestions on how to avoid this in future. As peers, maintain mutual respect by explaining that you appreciate the honest dialogue to gain a learning experience from this situation. Consistent with the employee conversation, ask what you could have done differently. If your peer seems to have a good amount of suggestions, position your follow-up question carefully to understand why these ideas weren't shared. You may comment on the validity and ask why these weren't shared before. Be sure to acknowledge that you want to be sure you are approachable on a team project, and would like to know if that impacted getting this feedback during the task. Finish by thanking your peer for his or her time and feedback, and follow up by indicating that you appreciate his or her expertise and appreciate getting ideas or suggestions for alternatives whenever possible. Your peer may be defensive about why he or she didn't approach you during the task, but keep in mind that you asked a simple question and maintained your professionalism. Any defensiveness is likely a sign of guilt or awareness that taking the silent route wasn't appropriate, and that is not your responsibility.

Hopefully defensiveness will not be what you experience when having this conversation with your manager. At the senior level, he or she should be comfortable providing feedback or communicating, so this conversation may be the most brief of all. Your manager is busy, that's a given, so providing this as a driving factor for unsuccessful delegation should be accompanied by suggestions for what could have been done differently. Minimal leading should be required, but remember to identify the failure and your role in that. Hopefully your manager will address the real question head-on, because he or she has lead these conversations and understands the thought process involved.

Let's evaluate the opposite reality—your manager admits no responsibility in the failure of the task. It's time to manage up. Stick to facts and ask the same probing questions from before—what could you, as the delegator, have done differently? If your manager finds no fault with you, it may be necessary to accept that you did your best, and the task was one of those growth opportunities. If your manager begins to rattle off a list of your shortcomings, ask the follow up question of why these weren't suggested during the assignment, or perhaps try asking if these ideas came to mind during or after the task. Take that feedback and close the conversation again with your appreciation for feedback. The fact is, your manager may have simply been distracted during the task, and simply powered through it with the objective of deadline over quality. Depending upon the feedback you receive from your conversation, you may become less likely to delegate to your manager, and there are several alternative options, so that is acceptable. The few tasks that need to be delegated up will stay the same, but you are otherwise open to other parties.

Although unpleasant, unsuccessful delegation means you gain insight about your list of potential delegates, as well as insight about yourself. Finding out how and where things went wrong is crucial to building the core ideas of delegation we have discussed throughout this book. Above all, do not look at unsuccessful delegation as a critical failure, even though it may be one in the short-term. Long-term, it is a teachable moment for everyone involved. Keep in mind the following concepts regarding unsuccessful delegation:

1. The task takes priority. If the failure is in quality or completion, rectify that situation prior to any feedback.

2. Reflect on your role in the unsuccessful outcome. Note what you could have done differently, including your choice of task, delegate, management of checkpoints, and communication of the assignment.

3. Meet with the delegate and ask probing questions.

4. Reinforce your openness to feedback and suggestions before, during, and after the process.

DELEGATING TO VOLUNTEERS

"The growth and development of people is the highest calling of leadership."

- Harvey S. Firestone

Delegation is a fine technique for getting things done where you have leverage over the delegate. In your management arsenal, you have tools for cajoling and rewarding your subordinates and to impose deadlines where necessary. In a volunteer situation, to have anything important accomplished, you have only what are commonly called "kid gloves."

The term "kid gloves" refers to gloves constructed of a very soft, smooth leather, and connotes gentle handling. This generally means that you must *persuade* and lead your volunteer to support your objectives. You, as a manager of a volunteer force, must do so from the perspectives of your volunteers' interests at least as much as from your personal or organization's interests.

In this chapter, we haven't much new to say on the subject of delegation itself—the activities are the very same as those detailed before—but the cohort and the audience of the delegate are radically different. It is now no longer possible simply to assign a task and expect it done. Even a carrot-and-stick approach isn't sufficient, as you are asking for a task to be completed and relying on the volunteer's interest and bonhomie to see it done.

If you wish to protect that volunteer force, you definitely don't want to micromanage it. There is nothing worse than finding someone bent on assisting you and then taking over the task yourself. A volunteer is, by definition, a self-motivated person. Anything that destroys that self-motivation will be detrimental to your operation.

It's important to recognize that a volunteer force is not simply free labor, a means to meet budget without obligating the organization for salaries and benefits. A volunteer force may have some of those benefits, but the rationale for involving volunteers is the attraction of common interests. It therefore follows that if your organization attracts a cadre of volunteers, it depends on its volunteers to be there, wishing to be used, and happy to be of service. That makes the management of these people crucial to the survival of the organization over time. For the want of a better term, let's call it "tender management."

People volunteer for a number of reasons. Having said that, please be aware of the single most important element of volunteerism: the satisfaction of the volunteer. In the simplest of terms, you attract a volunteer for many reasons, but the thing that keeps a volunteer involved in your activity will be his or her satisfaction with the effort— not yours.

Why do people volunteer at all? There are two forms of reason: intrinsic and extrinsic. Extrinsic motivations are those that are perceived as furthering coalescence with a group, gaining recognition, and providing protection. Intrinsic motivations will involve learning, development, and altruism.

Motivations are different according to age, gender, social status, and economic exposure, as well. A young, career ambitious worker might be motivated to become involved in volunteer activities that will provide an entrée to a career. This, for example, may be the motivation of a young woman who becomes a "candy striper," a volunteer worker at a hospital. It is also the motivation for a young person to take an unpaid position at a for-profit organization or in government as an intern. An older person may seek or accept a volunteer position as a means to keep busy, or to learn about how to care for a spouse. That person's motivation may be more to assist rather than to launch a bid for a next level of growth.

We do need, however, to identify two distinct types of volunteer, and the simplest label we can give them is "free" volunteer and "paid" volunteer (or employee). The free volunteer is in need everywhere: hospitals, child tutoring, workers at pet shelters, docents at museums, trail guides, readers at radio reading services. The list is limited only by the extent of your imagination, but the common factor is more a desire to be of service than to use that position for economic sustenance.

There is nothing wrong with being a paid volunteer. Many people with social service training fall into this category and the administration of group homes would be an impossibility otherwise. However, there is a second category of paid volunteer that we encounter, the *federated* volunteer.

There is no better example of the federated volunteer than the archetypes of the home businesses: direct marketing of products and services. Take, for example, the Avon dealer. An Avon dealer is attracted to the business by the ability to add to his or her income in the best possible way—by selling useful and necessary common items that deplete in a very short period. Avon's niche is largely cosmetics, as is Mary Kay's and a few others. Fuller Brush's is brushes and cleaning products. Watkins has spices. There are many more. There are legal services, communications services, transcription services—you name it. Recently, there has been a huge increase in weight management/fitness products such as ViSalus and AdvoCare. So long as an individual works at this independently, he or she obtains a slice of the price paid for the good or service, at least while the customer remains involved.

The federation process begins when an Avon dealer (or other) decides there is passive money to be made by attracting other dealers. Once certain minimums are met, the originating dealer is granted a percentage of the subordinates' sales. From that point on, the originating dealer is the manager of a volunteer force over which he or she has no organizational leverage. He can't fire her for nonperformance. Nor can he promote her within the organization. She can't cause the organization to produce additional benefits for her downline members. The company treats both as direct "independent" representatives, and the company makes all the rules.

What that means is that if the originating dealer wants to keep the benefits of the downline recruit, he or she must understand the motivation of that recruit and go to the utmost to support it. Sometimes, that isn't easy. The company that makes the rules is over all and the originating dealer is often held hostage for the shortcomings of the company itself.

What Attracts Volunteers?

The attraction for the federated volunteer is economic. Like it or not, a home-based business is *work*, and it is work with both internal and external pressures. There are people to see. There is product to obtain and pay for. The time given in the pursuit of "pushing" the product is not fully compensated. The one factor in its favor is the independence it affords, but even that is tossed by the wayside with the arrival of the least discouragement.

That's different from someone who has volunteered based on a strong interest or a love of subject. In this instance, the economic motivation is missing entirely. In its place must be the expectations of the volunteer relative to the activity of the volunteering itself.

If we can accept that motivation is the psychological need that activates a behavior, it would seem that understanding that behavior is the key to what a manager can delegate to that volunteer and what expectations can realistically be placed upon the volunteer.

For example, simply liking dogs is not a primary motivation for becoming involved in a pet shelter. In and of itself, liking dogs is a satisfying return for one's pet. What, then, would motivate a pet shelter volunteer to spend hours dealing with abused animals? Love for dogs— love to an extreme degree and the recognition that the volunteer has, or is willing to acquire, the skills to care for such animals.

The same must be true for caregivers, though many of those are compensated. The tasks lists are certainly comparable and the volunteers' commitments to those task lists imply the receipt of the responsibility, e.g., the delegation of duties.

In addition to the motivations to help, there are non-altruistic interests—such as leisure. The volunteer who exchanges the volunteer work for the ability to use the facility is an example of this. With this comes an interesting revelation—those who volunteer often do so with self-interest in mind. The availability of the interesting activity promotes the self-involvement beyond the volunteer activity. Thus, a former football player becomes involved with a Pop Warner league as a coach, or a radio amateur teaches a Morse code class.

Therefore, it may be that a combination of motivations drives the volunteer. Thus, a volunteer who subscribes to a specific value system may teach Sunday school, or the space engineer who has already made mathematics a career now provides tutoring services for calculus.

Who's to say that social motivations don't drive the force? How many times do people wish to attach themselves to someone from whom they know they can learn many things? The price is certainly right. If the volunteer has skills in one area, cannot he or she literally exchange those skills for the learning of skills in another area?

Rewards

It would be fair to say that reward is a driving motivation. Being number one at anything is a coalescing force for any group. It is the same for a volunteer group, and it isn't always important to some that the world knows it. An intrinsic knowledge of reward because of the activity of "helping others" may well drive an individual far more than a monetary award or recognition plaque given out at a banquet. However, the opposite is true also. Many want the plaque more than the money, or so they would tell you. In that case, the knowledge of others about the volunteer's involvement is more than sufficient exercise and rationale for the involvement.

However, rewards take several forms. For some, the personal development and learning, the gaining of new perspectives, or the addition of new experiences become driving forces, and sometimes that is accentuated by personal risk. Thus, Evel Knievel did motorcycle jumps, and Nick Wallenda does high-wire walks. There may be some compensation in endorsements for this, but the compensations of conquering danger are far more personal.

What about the rewards where the volunteering is just plain work —cleaning the bathrooms, mowing the lawn, peeling potatoes, doing the many things that a charge simply cannot do for himself. Where are those rewards? When that volunteer goes home at night, the rewards must lie squarely in the box marked, "I made a difference in somebody's life." *Do unto others as you would have them do unto you.*

Areas of Satisfaction

If I am to delegate to volunteers, I must be cognizant about the dimensions of volunteer satisfaction. These are myriad:

- Global satisfaction—is the volunteer happy with the assignment overall?

- Satisfaction with the volunteer experience—has the volunteer obtained sufficient emotional benefits from having done the work?

- Communication—is the volunteer satisfied with the quality and quantity of communication. Does he or she voice the need for additional information in order to perform the assigned tasks?

- Integration—does the volunteer feel a part of the organization during the period of his or her involvement? What does the volunteer feel about the organization itself?

- Satisfaction with the work—does the volunteer enjoy the work? Are there elements more enjoyable than others? Will the volunteer accept the less palatable tasks in exchange for the more palatable tasks?

- Satisfaction with you? If you are to manage a volunteer, is the person gaining from you in support of his or her motivation?

The Development and Retention of Volunteers

The training of a volunteer is seldom the issue. People volunteer in areas where they have at least some of the skills necessary to do the work. In federated volunteer activities, there is at least some informal training or the coaching necessary to meet the minimum effort requirements. If training is needed, then you, as the manager of the volunteer, must either provide it yourself or arrange for its provision.

There are two reasons for providing this training: (1) most people are eager to learn something new—to add to a skill set. People will volunteer where there is training, if for no other reason than to enhance the resume. That is one rationale for internships, after all, and

(2) people will stay where gaining in knowledge is an important activity.

To do this best, perhaps a survey of your volunteers is in order. Consider these as suggested reasons you will encounter (there may be more):

- Volunteering allows me to gain new perspectives.

- Volunteering allows me to learn new and interesting things.

- Volunteering increases my personal esteem.

- Volunteering helps me work through personal problems.

- I am meeting my personal objectives.

- I can do something for a cause that is important to me.

- I feel fulfilled professionally.

- I feel fulfilled personally.

- I enjoy other volunteers.

- I enjoy the interaction of my tasks with my clients.

- I can make contacts that will enhance my career.

- I can develop new skills that will be useful elsewhere.

What's in it for the Volunteer?

The list will provide insight. Nevertheless, consider these, as well:

- I can do a task I love to do without the pressure of paperwork.

- I can fit my volunteering to my personal schedule. I don't have to punch a clock.

- I can involve myself in an activity where I have no risk for doing it incorrectly.

- I can become involved in things that affect me emotionally.

- I can work where I see things to be done and can do them; I don't need to be directed.

- I can involve myself in the kind of activity where I never dreamed I had an interest.

- I can select the manager for whom I work.

- I can "get out of the house" or change my environment.

- I can strengthen my community.

- I enjoy the association of a group.

- I can learn things I never knew interested me.

- I see it as a civic responsibility.

- I can "pay it forward" or "give back."

- I can make a difference!

Volunteer Assessment

As a manager, just as you might assess the impact of a subordinate, you must also assess the impact of a volunteer. In the case of a volunteer, however, it isn't always an up or down decision. There are both competent and incompetent volunteers. Management of any kind of involvement is totally informal and unstructured, but that doesn't change the fact that there are areas of responsibility and reporting channels. At the same time, there may be other reasons of personal interest, not expressed during the interview, that cause a person's involvement in a volunteer assignment. Once that personal interest is satisfied, the volunteer disappears.

It is with the assessment of the impact of a volunteer that the kid glove treatments must be applied. There is a watchword for when that happens. It's when the interest is more personal than organizational. Often it happens that volunteers are recruited to "man the phones." You see that in every telethon. It is a good place to determine whether the volunteer ascribes to the reason for the activity. To be a volunteer at anything, there must be an emotional attachment and a stamina.

Why stamina? Volunteering at a pet shelter is an emotional task, and for a lover of animals, a labor of love. Consider what a volunteer at a hospice must encounter. Without the ability to handle stress and grief, a hospice volunteer simply wouldn't last very long.

The volunteer, like any other worker, likes to have a varied set of duties. Boredom is an enemy of any worker, but much more so for a volunteer, who can simply "chuck it" and find somewhere else to volunteer where the work and the people—and the organization—are far more interesting. It is acceptable for a volunteer to work outside his or her "comfort zone." Volunteers can continue personal and occupational growth, as well.

Advice for Managers of Volunteers

Since you have no organizational leverage over volunteers, what, then, might you do to enhance the volunteer experience and still have done what you have been tasked to do? Consider:

- Engage them in change. Organizations and their subdivisions change, and some of those changes will affect the role of the volunteer. Involve those volunteers in changes in mission or organization. Don't assume that simply because they are "unpaid staff" they will accept different circumstances.

- Extend the information distribution. Volunteers must be advised not only of their value, but must always receive the same information you would provide a paid employee.

- Provide a forum. Staff meetings should involve volunteers as well as paid staff. Give those volunteers a platform to be heard; listen to what they say. Often a volunteer has the same or better skills than an employee and generally has the years of experience necessary to make worthy contributions.

- Provide role definitions. You should have job descriptions for each employee. Should you not also have guidelines for volunteers? A volunteer may come to you willing to work but be unable to do so for the lack of training. Now you must decide whether the interest is strong enough to justify the underwriting of the training necessary to do the work.

- Establish the boundaries. In essence, draw your organizational chart to include volunteers. Not only is this a worthy guide for your volunteers to locate information, it also defines the relationships between staff members and volunteers.

- Learn about the people who volunteer. Nobody is asking you to socialize with your volunteers, but it wouldn't hurt. The issue is that you must deliberately learn about the individual's skills and strengths. There is a two-fold benefit for you in doing this: (1) it makes the volunteer feel valued, but it also (2) provides you with an index of untapped skill and experience resources, should they become useful.

- Keep it personal. Communicate in person. Stay away from group emails and impersonal text messages with your volunteers. People will come to see it as simply another chore. Granted, this is the electronic generation, but volunteers want intimacy with their volunteer situations. A phone call. An invitation into the office. A meeting at the water cooler. Find ways to keep it personal.

- Develop your volunteers. Always hold out the possibility of a career within the organization, or, failing that, offer a chance to move to other interesting volunteer assignments that may involve some schooling or training. A corollary to this is to allow the volunteer the opportunity to do what he or she has been trained to do.

- Seek the volunteer's opinion. You wish to know a number of things:

    1. Advisory: How might he or she handle a situation based on experience?

    2. Perspective: What would you change within the organization?

3. Opportunity: How may we use you most effectively?

4. Evaluative: What are your impressions of the organization?

5. Organizational: What would you change if you had the opportunity?

Manager's Cautions

Everything isn't quite as rosy as it would appear. There is a very narrow line between a volunteer and an employee when it comes to the appearance of the organization to the public. For example, does your volunteer interface with the public at large? If so, does he or she speak to the public on behalf of the organization? Do the customers and clients with whom the volunteer works perceive that their interface is a member of the organization itself?

Any employee of any organization has organizational rights. Among those are the rights to complain. A volunteer has a right to be treated equitably with any employees and consistently so. How can a volunteer ensure that a complaint is handled and resolved? Before you take on any volunteers, you need to consult counsel to ascertain a volunteer's rights within the organization.

This is the advice given by the Charities Review Council, drawn from the website (http://www.smartgivers.org/volunteer_rights_responsibilties):

As a volunteer, you have the right:

- To be treated as a co-worker, not just free help.

- To a suitable assignment—with consideration for personal preference, temperament, life experience, education and employment background.

- To know as much about the organization as possible—its policies, people and programs.

- To training for the job and continuing education on the job—including training for greater responsibility.

- To a job description.

- To a place to work—a designated place that is conducive to work and worthy of the job to be done.

- To new opportunities and a variety of experiences—through advancement or transfer, or through special assignment.

- To be heard—to feel free to make suggestions, to have a part in planning.

- To recognition—in the form of promotion and awards, through day-to-day expressions of appreciation and by being treated as a bona fide coworker.

- To sound guidance and direction.

There are responsibilities of a volunteer that accompany your rights as a volunteer. All of those involved in the relationship must have respect for one another and a desire to cooperate in meeting designated needs. Your responsibilities include:

- If you have criticism about another person, convey it to your supervisor.

- Be prompt and reliable in reporting for scheduled work. Keep accurate records of your hours worked.

- Notify your supervisor as early as possible if you are unable to work as scheduled.

- Attend orientation and training sessions scheduled.

- Be considerate, respect the ability of the staff, and work as a member of the team.

- Carry out assignments in good spirit and seek the assistance of your supervisor in any situation requiring special guidance.

- Accept the right of the agency to dismiss any volunteer for poor performance, including poor attendance.

- Decline work that is not acceptable to you; maintain an open mind with regard to other people's standards and values.

- Communicate personal limitations--acceptable out-of-pocket costs, transportation needs, time constraints, etc.

- Provide feedback, suggestions, and recommendations to your supervisor and staff if these might increase the effectiveness of the program.

- Give written notice if you cannot continue in your volunteer position or if you are requesting a leave of absence from the program.

- Have the ability to work with a culturally diverse population of clients.

- Respect current Council policies (i.e. Affirmative Action, Sexual Harassment, etc.).

Managing the Risk

Volunteers recognize that they are not hirelings. That is obvious. However, the existence of a volunteer force may become an issue where all or part of the hireling force is unionized. However, that is merely one consideration. Consider these also:

- Avoid anything that even smacks of a payment for volunteer work. If the volunteer incurs some expenses, pay those expenses precisely.

- You would be wise not to permit volunteers to handle money or establish contracts of any scope.

- Because you have a volunteer *position* defined, train to fit the position. The training must be seen as a necessity to do the volunteer assignment, not as a reward to induce the volunteer to make himself or herself available.

- Volunteers are not employees, and you have no leverage over them as employees, with the exception of the addition or removal of the person relative to the position. Therefore, define the relationship in terms of *expectations* instead of obligations.

- You might consider drafting (or having your legal support prepare) a volunteer agreement. This will identify the volunteer's role and is not enforceable as a contract.

- Revise the volunteer assignments periodically to alleviate boredom. Provide new opportunities to heighten interest and build your volunteer force. A volunteer training program is a worthy draw.

- Take action based on volunteer feedback; commend them for their feedback; allow them to take action within the scope of their volunteer assignments.

- Demonstrate to your volunteers periodically how their contributions have affected your organization and how they have made a difference by their presence.

Volunteers are valuable human resources. Many organizations couldn't do the good work that they do without their availabilities. The management of volunteers isn't significantly different from the management of direct employees, except for the special considerations that have been herein stated.

You may not be expected to keep every volunteer you recruit. It will be a revolving resource. Building volunteer management capacity to involve and retain them makes sense for any organization where there are needs that exceed the capacity of the paid staff to satisfy.

CONFESSIONS AND CONCLUSIONS

"I'm going from doing all of the work to having to delegate the work - which is almost harder for me than doing the work myself. I'm a lousy delegator, but I'm learning."

- Alton Brown

Now that we have concluded our discussion on delegation, you can seen the enormous power it holds to develop not only yourself as a leader but to enhance and encourage those around you. I am sure you have seen the recurrent themes of organization, prioritization, and communication in each of these chapters. It is imperative that these abilities are developed alongside your other delegation and leadership skills. If delegation is indeed the key to leadership as the title implies; then organization, prioritization, and communication are the keys to delegation.

These are not new concepts. If you pick up any good leadership book, I am sure you will find chapters devoted to each; in some cases, whole books have been penned on these topics. Likewise, leadership books will pay homage to delegation in some way, but in piecing this book together, I have found that delegation is essential to being a great leader, and it is important to focus on delegation as a central theme to leadership. Leaders can falter in certain skills (tech skills, speech writing, financial planning) but their strength lies in finding people who can do those things and do them better. As President Woodrow Wilson said, "I not only use all the brains that I have, but all I can borrow." *That* is the definition of delegation and the path of a true leader.

The notion that no one can do it better than me has to be stricken from your mindset. Gone is the idea that you don't have time to train or teach someone so it's easier to just do it yourself. You won't ever find the time (to train someone or for anything else) if you don't. You have to rely on others to be able to achieve all you want in life. Now, I know what you're thinking, "I do it all myself and I have everything I want."

Do you? Do you *really?* Do you have *enough* time with family and friends? for hobbies and leisure time? for (fill in the blank)? If you do, then great, but how did you get there? Did you start your own business? Did you invent a new life altering widget? If so, what are you doing now? Are you running every single aspect of the business? If the answer is no, then you had to delegate something somewhere. If the answer is yes, then you probably weren't honest about the answer to the above question about having enough time.

The problem with relying on others to get things done is the loss of control. If we delegate, then things may not go EXACTLY the way we thought. So what? Maybe it gets done bigger, better, or faster. If not, then it's back to the drawing board, but we will forget about all the other things we completed because we weren't concentrating on the thing that went south. The question is what do we really lose? The answer is ourselves! To quote Ozzy Osbourne "Of all the things I've lost, I miss my mind the most." Think about it. How many times have we overloaded our plates with tasks we could have delegated and ended up overworked, overstressed, over budget, and over deadline. We work late or bring it home and give up other things we would rather be doing. We lose our tempers with our spouse, kids, friends, or the random guy at the coffee shop. We get ulcers, gain weight, have heart attacks, and feel depressed. We end up justifying it by saying "I'm just too busy" or "I'm slammed at work." No you're not; you're just a bad delegator.

That last sentence brings me to the hardest part about this book: the confession. Here it is. Are you ready for this?

I did not write this book; I *delegated* this book.

Now before you throw it across the room, call me a fraud, and hold a book burning in the town square; let me explain:

As I mentioned in the introduction, several months before starting this book, I was as close to being clinically depressed as I could be without being properly diagnosed. Work was crazy; we were going through a restructuring and everyone feared the pink slip on a daily basis. Other things I was involved in seemed to be in a holding pattern, and I was always waiting on other people to do their part so I could do mine. My side business was requiring more and more of my attention. All of which fed that notion that I might as well do it myself if I wanted to make sure it was done right. I didn't have time to do this because of that, or because I worked late, or was on the road, or blah blah blah. I have a three year old and a one year old at home, so when I was bringing work home or working on other projects, I didn't have time to play with them, or I was frustrated at them because they would not be quiet and leave me alone so I could get my stuff done. I was at the end of my rope, and I was looking for answers anywhere I could find them.

I read "The 4-Hour Workweek" by Tim Ferriss and it gave me the insight/inspiration/kick in the pants I needed. I must admit, I had seen Tim's book before and brushed it off as one of those "get rich quick" schemes that plague the self-help section. It wasn't until my friend Chris Moore from Barbell Shrugged recommended it on Twitter that I finally decided to give it a chance. Honestly, if you haven't read it, please, PLEASE go pick it up. Not everything in there may be applicable to you (what book is?) but I can promise you will take something away from it that will impact your life. Many of the concepts in "The 4-Hour Workweek" ring back to the idea of finding ways to do things better and delegating out those tasks in order to make the amount of time you spend on a project minimal. Tim suggests finding a muse, a project that will fund an automatic income, in order to live life on your terms. For me, having the idea wasn't the hard part. I have lots of ideas; though, as my wife would say, some are good and some are pretty far out there. My problem was the step in between. How do I get from A to B if I don't necessarily have the skill set to get me there? Answer: DELEGATION

Anyway, back to me not writing this book. While making all these changes in my life, I decided I wanted to try a muse project like Tim suggested. This is where the book idea came from, but I'm not a good writer. (Some of you are probably thinking "Clay, you're still not a good writer.") In order to create my muse while also teaching myself to delegate tasks and be okay with the results, I assembled a team of writers, told them about the project, allowed their creative juices to flow, and turned them loose. I gave feedback, changed a few words, and added a paragraph here or there, but the majority of the book was written by the team.

Ultimately, this book was an experiment to see if I could apply the principles of delegation to an important project and reduce my overall stress level in other avenues of my life at the same time. I think it was a success. Not only have I learned things through the process of putting this book together but also the writers have given me a unique insight into delegation through their own experiences. Like Alton Brown, I'm still a lousy delegator; but I am working on it. At first, it was hard for me to give a writer a chapter title or idea and leave them to their own devices. I was nervous. Would they do a good job? Can they actually write a cohesive sentence? Do they have the experience to talk about delegation? Did I explain everything I wanted/needed to? Is this a dumb idea?

If we are all honest with ourselves, we ask the same types of questions. We question the abilities of others but also the ability of ourselves. If the person we delegate to is indeed incompetent, then we will look bad for choosing that person. If we do a poor job explaining and/or understanding the project, then we will look bad for our own incompetence. The last thing we want, in any circle we are associated with, is to look bad. So we justify the only option is to do it all ourselves... and we are back to where we were at the beginning of this chapter.

Hopefully, this book has given you the tools to make delegation easier and the confidence to step out on that limb and give some control up to others. It won't be easy and you will crash and burn. This book doesn't have all the answers but it will begin your journey or give you new ways to approach the same old problem. The important point is to keep trying, hone your skills, and become the leader you are meant to be. I leave you with these words from a man much smarter than I:

"Surround yourself with the best people you can find, delegate authority, and don't interfere as long as the policy you've decided upon is being carried out." - Ronald Reagan

ACKNOWLEDGMENTS

As I have confessed, I did not write this book entirely on my own. Additionally, we have discussed the importance of recognizing those to whom we delegate. With that in mind, I would like to thank the following people for their role in developing this book. I could not have done it without them:

Ken Lord

Victoria Eshghy

Janeane Moore

I hope you have both enjoyed and gained something from this book. If you have, please leave a review wherever you made your purchase. You can learn about upcoming projects and connect with the author via Twitter **@claymarlin** or via email: **thekeytoleadership@gmail.com**.

41720314R00075

Made in the USA
Charleston, SC
05 May 2015